FORF

IT WASN'T LONG after I had founded the Curry Club in 1982 that I received a membership enquiry from Perth in Western Australia. It was from one Joyce Westrip. I hadn't advertised in Australia, and I hadn't heard of Joyce, but in her typically thorough way she had heard of me. I soon got to know her and of her achievements. Born to British parents in Bangalore, Joyce is an Indophile, a true devotee of the world's most colourful, most irritating, most lovable country. She cooks, writes, reads, teaches, breathes and loves India and Indian food. Since then I've visited her home in Perth, and she's been to mine in England; we always have much in common to talk about.

Joyce lived for eighteen years in southern India and has revisited the subcontinent on numerous occasions. Indeed, she once came on one of my Gourmet Tours of India. Such trips can be very vexing, especially when otherwise educated and civilised beings choose to become the tour-leader's visitors from hell. For no good reason seven-star luxury becomes the subject of complaint. They decide that this and that are not to their liking – the rooms at the Sheraton Agra, the food at Delhi's Bukharra (the best tandoori restaurant in the world), the fact that fish has bones. And why does room service take so long to make samosas at 3 o'clock in the morning? On the group that Joyce was with, things came to a head when some members balked at giving a pathetic 100 rupees (about 70 pence) each as a tip to our coach-driver of ten days. Generosity is one of Joyce's hallmarks and she was far from being a complainant. In fact,

Joyce herself had led tour groups and, seeing frustration building up in me, she took me aside and made me laugh, telling of her experiences with irritating group members. On one occasion, after years of requests, she and her group were granted an audience with the then Prime Minister, Indira Ghandi. After her group left, an exalted Joyce talked of the great honour they had just received. She was met with surprise by some of the group, who thought that tea and cakes with the leader of the world's largest democracy was normal procedure for tour groups. On another occasion, her group was staying under canvas in the jungle near a hill station, as was clearly stated in their itineraries. Being quite unlike their seven-star hotel luxury, most were complaining as they went to bed in their tents. Joyce was prepared for such an eventuality. She always kept paper cups and a bottle of Scotch in her luggage. She poured generous measures and popped the cups through each tent flap, saying, 'Here's your medicine.' Next day a sheepish group appeared and peace broke out again.

'Fire and Spice' is an accurate description of Joyce on a mission as well as a very apt title for her book. It also sums up the Parsis and their cooking. Some years ago I was fortunate enough to take a short course in Parsi cookery at a college in Mumbai, which gave me an enduring delight in this unique cuisine as well as a wealth of Parsi friends in India and the UK. Foremost amongst them is Karan Billimoria who created Cobra Indian Beer in 1992 and built up the brand by delivering cases of lager to British curry houses from the back of a Citroën 2CV. Within a decade, he was turning over £50 million. He is absolutely typical of the Parsi drive that Joyce describes in her illuminating introduction. I went to Karan's wedding in Secunderabad, a typically Parsi affair, with 500 guests. Uniquely for India, the guests sit along one side of long tables, while numerous courses are served by waiters on the other side of the table. There is just one true Parsi restaurant in the UK; I wish there were more, but, as Joyce explains, Parsis are few in number. However, Joyce's assiduous researches and her Parsi-style drive have created this book, and we now have the opportunity to experience authentic Parsi food at home.

The little that most of us know about Parsi dishes is confined to what we glean from a two-liner at the curry house, where dhansak and patia are described on menus as 'Persian' dishes. And that, you might think, is that. But, as Joyce shows, there are dozens of Parsi recipes, whether for fish, pulses, meat or breads, using as wide a range of ingredients as may be found in any cuisine. *Fire and Spice* is a wonderful, confidently articulate, definitive cookbook. I can't think of a Parsi recipe which has been omitted. Joyce's historical facts are correct, and her recipes are unambiguous, clearly set out, and above all they work, something that cannot be said of all food writers.

If Parsi cooking is new to you, it is well worth exploring each and every recipe. And you'll have no better guide than Joyce Westrip.

Pat Chapman

ACKNOWLEDGEMENTS

FIRSTLY, I MUST THANK my husband Charles, without whose encouragement, patience and support this work could never have been undertaken. He was my constant companion in my travels and always keenly interested in my research.

This book is in no small part the result of the tolerance and guidance of my publisher and editor, Stephen Hayward. Hundreds of e-mails travelled back and forth between Australia and England, as Stephen patiently queried, questioned and prodded until we were both satisfied that things were as they should be. When he came across a particularly curly question, he was able to consult Maneck Suntook, Sherena Khan, Susie Dalal and Rachel Dwyer, to all of whom I am also very grateful.

My son Paul Hanlon and grandson Luke Hanlon acted as computer gurus, coming to my rescue on numerous occasions, while Stephanie Kukura typed and re-typed the recipes as the book took shape.

This book would never have been written without the initial help of Hazel Galbraith in Western Australia, Manize Sait in Singapore and the late Dorothy Sait in India. Thrity Kuka's central role in the book's genesis is explained in the Introduction.

In Mumbai the renowned caterer, writer and expert on all Parsi culinary matters, Katy Dalal, spent several hours explaining the finer points of Parsi cooking to me. Satish Arora, Director of Food Production and Chef Culinaire of the Taj Group of Hotels was most helpful. My friends Anil and Manek

Kadam, both now deceased, introduced me to many of their Parsi friends. Jasmine Kotval explained the navjote ceremony to me and even gave me photographs of her children, Xerxes and Nadine, at their navjote ceremonies. I was reassured by knowing that I could always reach out for advice from my friend the cookery writer Bapsi Nariman, while Pheroze Jungalwalla helped by putting me in touch with a variety of Parsi organisations. The staff of the Indian Tourist Offices in both Sydney and Mumbai were also very helpful.

There were many others who gave me help and encouragement. My sister Maureen Thomas was always there when I needed her good sense. Charmaine Solomon, an internationally acknowledged expert on Asian cuisines, was just a telephone call away. Charmaine Surin, Mercedes Webb-McDougall, Shakunthala Devagnanam, Margaret Fernandes, Peggy Holroyde, Aster Bapty, Nasim Bokhari, Rae Noble, David Weinman, Denise Young, Peter Lovejoy, Sushma Paul, Honorary Consul for India in Western Australia, cookery writer Sri Owen and her husband Roger, Pat Chapman, founder of the Curry Club, and his wife Dominique were all much appreciated sources of support.

INTRODUCTION

I WAS IN CENTRAL IRAN when the memory of a childhood meal was released by a chance encounter. Yazd, which sits at the crossroads of ancient caravan routes, is one of the last strongholds of Zoroastrianism in modern Iran and I was walking down a path lined by pomegranate trees towards the city's fire temple when I fell into conversation with some other travellers. They told me they were Parsis from Bombay who had come to visit the land of their ancestors. Parsis... Parsis... my memory whirred and all of a sudden I was a young girl eating lunch in a large, cool dining room belonging to friends of my parents in southern India.

As I enjoyed a spicy dhansak made with mutton and lentils, the head of the household told me that 'Parsi' means someone who comes from Pars, or ancient Persia. The old man was intensely proud of his heritage and explained to me that the Parsis are Zoroastrians, believers, like Jews and Christians, in a single god. More than a thousand years earlier in Persia, his ancestors had been persecuted for refusing to give up their faith, and so sought refuge in India.

He went on to tell his wide-eyed young guest about the Parsis' arrival in India. A group of refugees had sailed from Persia and landed on the island of Diu, near Cambay. A few years later an astrologer priest advised them to move to the land of a benevolent ruler. They set sail again and landed at Sanjan on the coast of what is now the state of Gujarat. Three of their *dasturs*, or priests, approached the Hindu King Jadi Rana for permission to stay and requested a grant of land. Jadi Rana was a generous ruler, but he felt that he needed to protect his people from intruders. He shook his head and indicated that there was no room in his land by filling a vessel with milk to the point of overflowing. One of the *dasturs* stepped forward and sprinkled some sugar into the almost overflowing bowl, suggesting that there was still room and that the milk – or the land – could be enhanced with the judicious addition of a new element. The king was so impressed by this subtle approach that he gave permission for the refugees to remain, granting them land and freedom of worship under certain conditions. The first fire temple on Indian soil was built at Sanjan, and the fire kindled there has been the parent fire for all the other fire temples in India.

I was in Iran researching the Persian influence on India's Moghul cooking when I met the Parsis making a pilgrimage to Yazd, and speaking to them alerted me to the fact that Persian techniques, ingredients and flavourings had entered India long before the arrival of the Moghuls in the sixteenth century. The Parsis who were given permission to settle by Jadi Rana had brought with them a cuisine that a millennium later still contains many recognisably Persian elements. The memory of that dhansak eaten in Bangalore forty years earlier flooded back, my interest in the Parsis was reawakened and I decided to look into Parsi as well as Moghul cookery.

On my next visit to India I began to make some initial enquiries about Parsi cooking, but was soon frustrated by my failure to track down books on the subject. When I told the renowned Bombay chef Satish Arora of my problems he pointed me in the direction of a second-hand bookshop stacked from floor to ceiling with well-thumbed volumes. I found several books on the history of the city's Parsi community, but only one on Parsi cooking, Jeroo Mehta's *101 Parsi Recipes*. The bookseller said that he was unaware of any other English-language books on the subject, although I was later to discover that there were in fact a couple of other Parsi cookbooks. As I was leaving the hotel for the airport the next day I was given a note from Satish with a list of 100 Parsi dishes.

My first task was to get the recipe titles translated from the Parsi dialect of Gujarati into English. Hazel Galbraith, a friend in Australia, told her sister in Madras about my problem, and she contacted Manize Sait, her Parsi sister-in-law, who lives in Singapore. Manize, in turn, put me in touch with her cousin in Bombay, Thrity Kuka.

I had no idea that making contact with Thrity would prove to be a major turning point. Thrity sent me an English trans-lation of Satish's list of recipes and in the same letter mentioned, almost as an afterthought, that she had inherited two handwritten books containing hundreds of recipes dating back to the 1860s. We came to an agreement and Thrity agreed to translate her family recipes into English and help me with adapting and testing them for use in modern kitchens. Thrity sent me the recipes, interspersing them with information about Parsi rituals and culture and drawings of cooking utensils. For three years letters flew back and forth between India and Australia. Twice during that time we met in Bombay, and on both occasions I learned yet more about Parsi food and customs. For Thrity, the translation was a mammoth task, and not just a linguistic one – recipes referred to an *anna*'s worth of coriander, while other measurements were given in *tolas* and *seers* and had to be converted to metric and imperial quantities. *Fire and Spice* is the result of our joint labours and Thrity and I remain good friends.

The conditions imposed by Jadi Rana included the wearing of saris by Parsi women, the surrender of all weapons and the adoption of the Gujarati language. The Zoroastrian newcomers also promised not to attempt to convert others to their religion and to respect the sentiments of their neighbours by not slaugh-tering cows, which Hindus regard as sacred.

Zoroastrianism is the world's oldest monotheistic religion and many of its doctrines, including that of the Last Judgement, have been adopted by other faiths. It takes its name from the prophet Zarathushtra, who was known as Zoroaster to the ancient Greeks. Zoroastrians do not believe in reincarnation, so it is important that man becomes master of his own destiny during his time on earth. Zoroastrians are expected to work towards the triumph of good over evil, and are responsible for their own actions and for the fate of their souls. Devout Zoroastrians strive to be honest and charitable, and, above all, to lead active and industrious lives. The most important religious rituals are purification ceremonies involving fire, which symbolises purity and truth. Zoroastrians are not, as some people believe, fire worshippers, but because fire is sacred, like earth and water, neither burial nor cremation is an option for them. Bodies are placed in Towers of Silence, or *dakhmas*, and exposed to the sun and air. Birds, usually vultures, dispose of the flesh and the sun dries the bones, which quickly turn to powder. Parsis believe this method of disposal of corpses to be both hygienic and egalitarian, as the bodies of rich and poor are disposed of in an identical manner.

The promise not to proselytise made to Jadi Rana some ten centuries ago has contributed to a steep decline in Parsi numbers in recent years. Modern Parsi families tend to be small, and the latest estimate is that the community in India numbers about 60,000; according to the 1951 Census, there were then 111,791 Parsis living in the country. The law against conversion has been relaxed and today it is possible to convert to Zoroastrianism, but those who do so do not thereby become Parsis. In earlier times a Parsi who married a non-Parsi was considered an outcast, as was any offspring of that union. This ruling has been relaxed, and today the child of a Parsi father can be admitted to the faith and embraced as a member of the Parsi community. However this is not the case for the children of a Parsi woman who marries a non-Parsi, and there have been campaigns to overturn this law and give the children of such marriages the same right to initiation into the faith, to be invested with the *sudra* and *kusti*, the sacred shirt and the sacred thread, and to worship at the fire temples. Emigration to Britain, Canada and Australia is another factor that has contributed to the dwindling numbers; younger Parsis, away from the strict confines of their community in India, no longer adhere to the rigid rules on marriage that bound their parents in India.

Parsis tend to place great value on education, and as one of the most literate communities in India over the centuries they have found employment as interpreters and negotiators for rulers, traders and invaders alike. When Akbar, the Moghul emperor, conquered Gujarat in 1573, he became interested in the Parsi community living there. Their origins, after all, were in Persia and, for the Moghuls, Persia was the fount of culture. At the time, the emperor was trying to create a new universal religion and his court at Fatehpur Sikri became a centre of debate between invited religious leaders, including Hindus, Catholic missionaries from Goa and Dastur Meherji Rana, who represented the Parsis. Akbar was opposed by the mullahs and failed in his attempt to form a new religion, but Parsi priests acquired additional status in the aftermath of this event.

Although some Parsis living in the coastal town of Surat had played the role of interpreters and go-betweens for the Portuguese and the British, a new era in the community's history began with the rise of the East India Company and its decision to shift its interests from Surat to Bombay. The ascendancy of the British Raj witnessed the arrival of Parsis in positions of prominence in the fields of politics, commerce, education and culture. The catalyst was education.

The Elphinstone Institution (later Elphinstone High School and Elphinstone College) was founded in Bombay in 1834 'to instruct [Indians] in languages, science, literature and the philosophy of Europe' so that they could act as go-betweens with the vast population ruled by the British. The proportion of Parsis who attended far exceeded their Hindu counterparts and they quickly acquired the skills that prepared them for administrative roles. It was not long before they created their own educational institutions, which were soon turning out a Parsi-dominated Indian middle class. By 1882 there were Parsi judges, magistrates, revenue officers, bankers, engineers, industrialists, surgeons and politicians. This small community went on to make a contribution to India out of all proportion to its size.

Sir Jamsetji Jeejeebhoy was the first Indian director of the Great Indian Peninsula Railway and did much to improve facilities for the poor by having wells sunk and bridges built in the villages of Gujarat. He founded Bombay's first civilian hospital, and also the Jamsetji Jeejeebhoy School of Art, today recognised as one of the finest institutions of its kind in India.

Sir Cawasji Jehangir Readymoney, who became Income Tax Commissioner in 1860, provided water for the poor by sinking wells and erecting drinking fountains throughout Bombay. He also built a hospital at Surat, an ophthalmic hospital at Byculla, the Civil Engineering College at Poona and the neo-gothic Elphinstone College building in Bombay itself.

No survey, however brief, of Parsi achievements in the world of business can ignore Jamsetji Tata, of whom Lord Curzon said, 'No Indian of the present generation has done more for commerce and industry than Mr Tata.' In 1868 he founded the House of Tata, which rapidly became the country's largest private company, touching almost every aspect of Indian life. Jamsetji Tata is widely recognised as the creator of India's steel industry, and he also gave Bombay its first luxury hotel, the Taj Mahal, the first building in the city to be lit by electricity. His interest in Bombay's affairs was instrumental in the city building modern municipal housing for its citizens. He also played a key role in persuading the municipality to reclaim malarial swamps and develop them into the modern suburbs of Bandra, Mahim and Juhu Tara. A man of great vision, Jamsetji Tata gave India its first scientific institution, the Indian Institute of Science at Bangalore. The House of Tata went from strength to strength with the help of his sons, Dorab J. and Sir Ratan J. Tata, and his

nephew J.R.D. Tata, acquiring interests in iron and steel, loco-
motives, trucks, buses, engineering, chemicals, pharmaceuticals,
insurance, electronics and aircraft. Tata Airlines, founded in
1932, became Air India International in 1948; it was the first
joint undertaking between the government and the private
sector and was nationalised in 1953. The family's financial
success is reflected in the pioneering trusts, including the Tata
Institute of Social Sciences, the Tata Memorial Hospital for
Cancer and the Tata Institute of Fundamental Research, it has
established over the years. Initially these were communal in
nature, benefiting only Parsis, and limited to medicine and the
sciences, but today they serve all sections of the population and
also fund the arts and humanities. J.R.D. Tata ruled over the
family's business empire for five decades. In 2002 the Tata Group
celebrated the centenary of Mumbai's Taj Mahal Hotel. Today,
India's largest private sector group continues to flourish under
the chairmanship of another member of the family, Ratan Tata.

The Parsi community produced some of the most remarkable
people in India's history. Lowjee Nusserwanji, founder of the
great shipbuilding company, Wadia, built some three hundred
ships between 1735 and 1863. Bombay Parsis formed a cricket
club in 1848 and a few years later Dr M.E. Pavri captained the
first Indian cricket team to visit England. Mehli Mehta founded
the Bombay Philharmonic Orchestra and his son Zubin is an
internationally famous conductor. A Parsi doctor founded the first
maternity home in Bombay. The first Indian-owned newspaper
in the English language, the *Bombay Chronicle*, was launched by
Pherozeshah Mehta, who was dubbed 'the uncrowned King of
Bombay' for his work and leadership on the Bombay Corporation,
in the Congress and on the Imperial Legislative Council. He
later became Vice-Chancellor of Bombay University.

Both at home and abroad, Parsis were prominent in politics
as well as in business. In 1892 Dadabhoy Naoroji, the
Conservative member for Finsbury Central, became the first
Indian MP at Westminster, while Shapurji Saklatvala was the

Communist MP for Battersea in the 1920s. Parsis were also politically active in the subcontinent and closely associated with the movement for India's independence from British rule.

Parsi women have been pioneers in a number of fields. Vera Katrak, the first woman to obtain a doctorate in archaeology from London University, Perin Jamshedji Mistri, India's first woman architect and Lady Sherene Dinshaw Petit, the country's first female pilot, were all Parsis, while Mehri Tata formed India's first Council of Women, which brought women of different castes and creeds together and in 1923 became part of the International Council of Women.

Jamshed Aga, the first Indian to serve on the Council of the Royal Institute of British Architects and Sir Dadiba Merwanji, India's first High Commissioner in the United Kingdom, were both Parsis, as was Aspy Engineer, who made the first solo flight between England and India and went on to become an Air Marshall. Sam Manekshaw, now in his eighties and living in the Nilgiri Hills, the architect of India's victory in the 1971 war against Pakistan, was later appointed Field Marshall and is probably the country's best known Parsi soldier.

Whilst much has been written about the community's business, political and other achievements, relatively little has been written about the Parsi contribution to India's culinary traditions. Parsi recipes are included in works on Indian cooking, but only a handful of books have been devoted specifically to the subject. In my collection of almost 1,000 volumes on the cooking of the subcontinent, only four writers, Bapsi Nariman, Jeroo Mehta, Bhicoo J. Manekshaw and Katy Dalal, have written books about Parsi cooking.

The Parsis were Persians and had remained so, to a large degree because of their strict rules on marriage within the community. They also retained particular food habits for certain ceremonies and rituals, such as serving the sweet dishes Ravo and Sev on auspicious occasions. Recipes naturally become somewhat Indianised with the use of local spices and ingredients such as coconut and tamarind, yet they have retained an individuality that became known as the Parsi style. The Moghuls adapted some Parsi dishes, most notably *khichri* (for which the Parsi name is *khichdi*) in which rice and pulses are cooked together, sometimes with the addition of fruit and nuts – see, for example, Orange-Flavoured Rice with Dates (p.132). One or two Western influences have found their way into Parsi cooking as a result of the contact with members of the British Raj. Flavours are intensified with the use of Worcestershire Sauce and other European ingredients, such as hard cheese, and it is thought that the custards so popular with Parsis were adapted from the cooking of Anglo-India. The Parsis have contributed greatly to the Indian way of life and not least to its culinary arts.

India is a vast land and her cuisines have evolved over the centuries in a number of widely differing environments. The cool mountain regions of the Himalayas and the Vale of Kashmir produce hard fruits like apples and pears and stone fruits such as apricots and peaches, as well as walnuts and almonds used to thicken sauces, while lambs and goats are fattened on highland pastures. In the fertile valleys and rich alluvial plains of northern India basmati rice flourishes alongside wheat, millet, corn and vegetables. The country's rivers, streams and oceans are home to hundreds of varieties of fish and shellfish. In the south and west of the country, coconuts and tropical fruits such as banana, mango and pawpaw grow alongside fields of rice and pulses. From those regions too come chillies, pepper, cardamom, cloves and other spices, together with okra and herbs such as coriander and fenugreek. This abundance and variety of ingredients, together with regional and cultural differences have contributed to the diverse culinary history of the subcontinent.

Western India embraces Gujarat, the site of the first Parsi settlement in India, and Maharashtra, with Bombay as its capital, where the majority of Parsis have lived since the eighteenth century. Most of Maharashtra lies on the Deccan

Plateau; it is largely agricultural, with coconut palms fringing the coastal strip where the king of mangoes, the Alphonso, is eagerly awaited in the summer months. Parsis love fish, and the salt fish known as Bombay Duck is a particular favourite. On the whole, Parsis are not great eaters of vegetables, instead favouring fruits and nuts such as pomegranates, dates and almonds as ingredients to be combined with meats and pulses.

The Zoroastrian religion provides many excuses for social gatherings, as ceremonies and rituals are often followed by feasting, with particular dishes served on specific occasions. Dhansak, a dish of lamb or chicken cooked in a lentil and vegetable purée, is served on days when ancestors and departed souls are remembered. There are special dishes prepared for the mother of a newborn child. For four days after the birth the mother is restricted to a very light diet. On the fifth day she has to have a taste of seven dishes which must comprise lamb, chicken, fish, two or three types of offal, including brains, and a bread. When the child is able to sit up, it is given its first solids of rice and lentils. At the age of seven, the *navjote* ceremony initiating the child into the Zoroastrian faith takes place. The child is invested with the sacred thread and the sacred shirt, and sprinkled with rose petals, rice and pomegranate seeds, which symbolise fertility. The fruit or the leaves are an important offering, along with other ingredients such as coconut, rice, dates and nuts.

On special occasions it is quite common for large numbers of guests to be invited, especially for the *lagans*, or wedding receptions, and for the feast following the *navjote* ceremony. These are usually catered functions and are often held in a garden setting or in hotels. Traditionally, the food is served on large individual banana leaves, but nowadays plates are taking over. The order in which the food is served is more or less fixed, starting with a pickle, followed by a bread and a type of wafer, then fish, followed by chicken and then lamb, often in the form of cutlets or kebabs. No Parsi feast wedding feast would be considered complete without eggs, which are served fried or scrambled. The last of the savoury dishes tends to be chicken liver and gizzard, but this is by no means the end of the feast; the traditional rice, pilau or biryani, is served often with lentils; finally ice-cream and wedding custard are served.

Ceremonies are performed over several days before the actual wedding takes place, and each event involves food in one way or another, either as an offering or part of a ritual or as refreshment. Foods used at weddings include coconut, rice, wheat, eggs, turmeric, betel leaves, mung beans, dates, almonds, sugar, fish and yoghurt.

The Parsi new year falls in March and is celebrated with friends and relations over lunch and dinner. Guests are greeted by a long table onto which certain significant items are placed, including vinegar, spices, herbs, fruit, garlic, sugar, milk, sweetmeats, honey and painted eggs and a pomegranate or leaves from the pomegranate tree. The room is perfumed with sandalwood and incense. The meal normally includes rice, lentils, a sweet and sour fish curry and a vegetable dish, which are normally followed by Ravo, a sweet semolina pudding (p.161).

When a loved one dies, the *oothamma* ceremony takes place, and foods such as pomegranates, dates, milk and sometimes wine and a thick chapati known as darun are presented to the priest. As with marriage, there are many ceremonies and rituals performed when a person dies. Prayers are also recited over meals for four days after death takes place. Parsis believe that the soul of the dead person remains around their loved ones for three days. On the fourth day the legendary meal of dhansak, the dish that introduced me to Parsi cuisine all those years ago, is served with kebabs, brown rice, Kachubar and mango chutney.

MEAT DISHES

THE ZOROASTRIAN RELIGION imposes no prohibition on the eating of any particular type of meat, but Parsis living in India refrain from eating beef out of respect for their Hindu neighbours. For the majority community, cows are sacred and beef is forbidden, even to those whose faith allows them to eat meat.

Pork, of course, is abhorrent to India's Muslim minority, but it is not forbidden to meat-eating Hindus or Christians and is very popular in Goa, where a significant proportion of the population is Roman Catholic as a result of four centuries of Portuguese rule, and I have enjoyed a delicious Pork Vindaloo, a recipe of Goan origin, at the home of Parsi friends. Large pig farms are to be found in various parts of India and it is quite common to see scrawny-looking pigs foraging for food by the roadside. Of the relatively few pork recipes in the Parsi culinary repertoire, I include one for Pork Curry on p.43, a sweet and sour dish that makes a change from the lamb dishes that tend to dominate Parsi meat cookery.

In most of India – except Kashmir, where lamb is king – sheep are slaughtered only when they have reached a certain age. Mutton is preferred to lamb because it stands up to a longer cooking time, thus allowing the flavours of herbs and spices to penetrate the meat more fully, although more kid, or young goat, is consumed in India than any other meat. For the health-conscious, kid has the advantage of being leaner than lamb or mutton, and it doesn't have the rank odour sometimes associated with the meat of older members of its species. If goat isn't easily obtainable, young lamb, sometimes called milk-fed lamb, may be substituted. Any cut of lamb may be used in the recipes that follow. I have stipulated lean lamb, but in most Indian households the meat would not be trimmed of all its fat, which enriches the flavour of whatever dish it forms a part.

KID WITH POTATOES

Papeta Ma Kid Gosht

A selection of Parsi meat dishes would be incomplete without at least one recipe calling for kid. Here the young goat meat is rubbed with ginger and garlic and left to marinate. The meat is then fried and added to potatoes and tomatoes in an aromatic masala – a combination of spices – made with cinnamon, cardamom and cloves. If you cannot find kid, young lamb makes an acceptable substitute. Young goat rubbed with a ginger and garlic paste is delicious when cooked in a barbecue kettle or on a spit over a wood fire.

1 kg/2 lb kid, cut into 5 cm/2 inch cubes
8 cm/3 inches finely chopped ginger
3 cloves finely chopped garlic
2 tbsp ghee

Put the cubed meat into a bowl and rub in the ginger and garlic. Set aside for 1 hour. After marinating the kid, heat the ghee and fry the meat to seal it. Set aside.

---

4 tbsp ghee
2 finely sliced large onions
2 tsp chilli powder
2 cinnamon sticks
10 cloves
10 light-coloured cardamom pods, bruised
20 peppercorns
2 large tomatoes, chopped
3 large potatoes, diced
1 cup water
1 tsp salt or to taste
1¹/₂ cups canned coconut milk

Heat the ghee in a heavy-bottomed pan, fry the onions until they start to change colour, add the chilli powder, cinnamon sticks, cloves, cardamoms and peppercorns and fry for about 3 minutes to release their aromas. Add the tomatoes, potatoes and water and bring to the boil.

Mix in the meat with any liquid that has accumulated. Add salt and simmer for 5 minutes, remove from the heat and pour in the coconut milk. Return to the heat and continue cooking until the meat is tender – this will probably take between 1 and 1¹/₂ hours.

LIGHTLY-SPICED LAMB STEW

Sali Boti

Easy to prepare, this delicately spiced dish has a touch of sweetness and is ideal for everyday eating. It is best served with lentils or vegetables and rice or bread. Potatoes cut into pieces little larger than matchsticks are known as potato straws or *sali* in Parsi cooking. They are fried until crisp and golden and may be cooked ahead and, when cold, stored in an airtight container. I often prepare the straws in larger quantities than called for in the recipe and put some aside to serve with drinks.

3 tbsp vegetable oil
2 finely sliced onions
4 cm/1¹/₂ inches grated ginger
4 cloves finely chopped garlic
1 tsp cumin seeds
1 tsp chilli powder
1 tsp garam masala
1 tsp turmeric powder

Heat the oil in a heavy-bottomed pan. Fry the onions until they start to change colour, then add the ginger, garlic and cumin seeds and fry for 2 minutes. Add a little water if the mixture is inclined to stick. Then add the chilli powder, garam masala and turmeric and stir-fry for 1 minute.

1 kg/2 lb cubed lean lamb
Salt to taste
1 tsp soft brown sugar

3 large tomatoes, puréed
1 cup water
1/2 cup yoghurt

Add the meat, salt and sugar to the above mixture and fry to seal. Add the puréed tomatoes, water and yoghurt and bring to the boil. Then reduce the heat and simmer for approximately 1 hour or until the meat is cooked and tender. Remove to a serving dish and garnish liberally with crisp potato straws.

---

2 large potatoes, peeled
2 tsp salt
Vegetable oil for deep-frying

Cut the potatoes into pieces the size of large matchsticks. Place them in a large bowl, sprinkle with salt, cover with cold water and leave to sit for 15 minutes. Drain, spread the potato straws onto a tea towel and pat dry, absorbing as much moisture as possible. Heat the oil in a deep pan or fryer. When the oil begins to splutter, add the potato straws in batches and fry until golden and crunchy. Remove with a slotted spoon and drain on absorbent paper.

SWEET AND SOUR LAMB

Gosht Na Curry Chawal

This is a full-bodied dish, its sauce made rich with cashews, poppy seeds, coconut and tomatoes, and the addition of potatoes to the meat makes a hearty meal when served with plain rice. Tamarind pulp is available in compressed block form, which is slightly sweeter than the paste or concentrate. Tamarind paste and concentrate are available from oriental stores and some supermarkets and may be more convenient to use. If you are using the paste or concentrate, dilute 1¹/₂ tablespoons of the paste or 3 teaspoons of the concentrate in 1 cup of hot water.

175 g/6 oz tamarind pulp
1¹/₂ cups hot water

Soak the tamarind pulp in the hot water. When the water has cooled, squeeze and rub the pulp with your fingers to dissolve the tamarind. Strain through a sieve and retain the liquid, discarding the seeds and fibres. Set aside.

8 cloves garlic
2.5 cm/1 inch ginger

Add a little water to the garlic and ginger and blend to a paste.

3 tbsp ghee or vegetable oil
2 finely sliced onions
2 tsp coriander powder
2 tsp cumin powder
1 tsp turmeric powder
1 tsp chilli powder
2 tsp roasted and ground poppy seeds
1 tbsp roasted and ground cashews
¹/₄ can drained chick-peas
30 g/1 oz freshly grated or desiccated coconut
750 g/1¹/₂ lb cubed lean lamb
3 large potatoes, quartered
2 large tomatoes, chopped
2 tsp soft brown sugar

1 tsp salt or to taste
2 cups hot water

Heat the ghee or oil in a heavy-bottomed pan, fry the onion and the paste until the onion starts to change colour, stirring to prevent sticking. Add the coriander, cumin, turmeric, chilli, poppy seeds, cashews, chick-peas and coconut. Stir-fry the mixture for 3 minutes, adding a little water if the mixture is inclined to stick. Add the lamb and potatoes and stir to coat. When the meat is sealed, add the tomatoes, sugar, tamarind extract, salt and hot water. Reduce the heat and simmer until the meat is tender. This will take between 1 and 1¹/₂ hours. Serve with plain white rice and Coconut Chutney (p.171).

LAMB WITH APRICOTS

Jardaloo Ma Boti

Mutton may be used instead of lamb in this simple but flavour-some recipe. Dried figs and sometimes cubes of fresh pineapple are added to – or substituted for – the apricots. When I was first served this dish, my Parsi friends were quick to point out that the use of apricots indicates that this is a recipe of Persian origin. If you are arranging a meal by courses, serve this fairly dry dish with one of the breads as a starter or first course.

1¹/₂ tbsp ghee
1 finely chopped onion
3 cloves finely chopped garlic
4 cm/1¹/₂ inches finely chopped ginger

500 g/1 lb lean lamb, cubed
2 cups water
Salt to taste

Heat the ghee in a heavy-bottomed pan. Fry the onion, garlic and ginger until the onion starts to change colour, then add the meat and fry until it is sealed. Add the water and salt and simmer until the meat is cooked and the liquid has almost evaporated – this can take between 1 and 1½ hours. Remove to a serving dish and keep warm.

---

2 tbsp sugar
½ cup water
125 g/4 oz dried apricots, slivered

Put the sugar, water and the dried apricots into a heavy-bottomed saucepan and simmer until the apricot slivers are softened. To serve, spoon the fruit and liquid over the meat.

SPICY KEBABS

Kabab

Dhansak (p.38) takes pride of place in Parsi cooking. It is a wholesome meal of lamb cooked with lentils and vegetables and always served with spicy kebabs, a salad and a sweet mango accompaniment. These kebabs are a perfect companion to drinks, especially when served with one of the numerous sauces to be found on the shelves of supermarkets and oriental stores. I find that a sweet chilli sauce goes particularly well with these kebabs or, if you prefer a cooling effect, add some finely chopped fresh mint and coriander leaves to natural yoghurt. If made a little larger, the kebabs can be served with a salad as a first course.

---

500 g/1 lb minced lean lamb
1 finely chopped onion
4 cm/1¹/₂ inches finely chopped ginger
1 clove finely chopped garlic
2 finely chopped green chillies
2 tsp coriander powder
1 tsp cumin powder
1 tsp garam masala
1 tbsp finely chopped coriander leaves
1 tbsp finely chopped mint
¹/₂ tsp ground black pepper
2 tsp lemon juice
4 slices stale bread, crusts removed, soaked in water and squeezed of moisture
Salt to taste

Mix all the ingredients together in a bowl. Knead the mixture well. Then moisten your hands, form the mixture into small balls and flatten them into pattie shapes. Refrigerate for 1 hour to firm up the patties.

Vegetable oil for shallow frying

Heat the oil and gently fry the kebabs on each side until cooked. This should take 2–3 minutes each side.

LAMB WITH OKRA

Tarela Bhida Ma Gosht

Okra is often called 'lady's fingers' because it is supposed to resemble slender tapered fingers. Large okra pods tend to be stringy and tough, so try to select small, young pods that are bright green in colour. A good way to test for freshness is to snap the end near the tip – if it breaks off easily, the okra is tender.

500 g/1 lb okra
3–4 tbsp ghee
1 finely chopped onion
5 cm/2 inches finely chopped ginger
1 clove finely chopped garlic
1 tsp ground black pepper
1 tsp turmeric
500 g/1 lb cubed lean lamb
3 cups meat or vegetable stock or water
Salt to taste

Tail and cut the okra into 2.5 cm/1 inch lengths. Heat the ghee in a heavy-bottomed pan, toss and fry the pieces of okra for about 1 minute, then remove with a slotted spoon and set aside. Fry the onion, ginger and garlic in the remaining ghee until the onion starts to change colour. Then stir in the black pepper and turmeric, add the meat and continue frying until it is sealed. Pour the water or stock over the mixture, add the salt and simmer for about 1 hour until the lamb is tender and the liquid much reduced. Gently stir in the okra pieces and cook for about 2–3 minutes. The okra should be tender but slightly crisp. Over-cooking will cause the okra to become slimy and mushy.

DEEP-FRIED LAMB KEBABS

Kabab Gostna Tarela

Lamb kebabs flavoured with mint, fresh coriander and black pepper are coated in semolina and then deep-fried. They make a delicious snack and go well with pre-dinner drinks.

4 cm/1¹/2 inches roughly chopped ginger
10 cloves garlic
¹/2 cup mint leaves
1 cup coriander leaves
3 green chillies
2 tbsp lime or lemon juice

Blend the ginger, garlic, mint and coriander leaves, chillies and lime or lemon juice to a smooth paste.

500 g/1 lb finely minced lean lamb
2 tsp ground black pepper
1¹/2 tsp salt
1 tsp turmeric
¹/4 cup yoghurt, drained of whey

Put the minced lamb into a bowl with the pepper, salt, turmeric and yoghurt. Add the blended paste and mix well to integrate all the ingredients. Cover and refrigerate for 1 hour so that the mixture becomes firm.

1 lightly beaten egg
1 cup semolina to coat the kebabs

Vegetable oil for deep-frying

After refrigeration, knead the beaten egg into the mixture. Moisten your hands lightly and form the mixture into walnut-sized balls. Spread the semolina onto a flat surface and roll the kebabs in the semolina until they are well coated.

Deep-fry the kebabs a few at a time. Remove with a slotted spoon and drain on absorbent kitchen paper.

LAMB WITH VEGETABLES AND LENTILS

Farmasso Dhansak Ni Dal

'Farmasso' means 'first rate' or 'excellent'. This dish is a complete meal of meat, vegetables and lentils served with Caramelised Spicy Rice (p.117), Spicy Kebabs (p.34) and accompanied by Kachubar, a typical Parsi salad (p.175), and Aambakalio, a sweet mango dish (p.173). It is often served on a day when ancestors and departed souls are remembered. The traditional recipe is intended to be fiery hot as it calls for both red and green chillies. When I was given this recipe, 7 green and 10 red chillies were recommended. I have reduced the quantities of chillies used, but you may wish to increase the heat by adding more.

250 g/8 oz toovar (pigeon pea) lentils
1 can cooked and drained chick-peas

Rinse the lentils until the water runs clear. Place in a bowl, cover with water and set aside to soak for 4 hours or overnight. Drain. Rinse and drain the canned chick-peas.

———————

2 diced potatoes
250 g/8 oz diced pumpkin
1 small diced aubergine
1 tbsp chopped fenugreek leaves
1 diced white radish
1 cup roughly chopped coriander leaves
3 finely chopped green chillies
^{1}/$_2$ cup chopped mint leaves
1^1/$_2$ tsp turmeric
2 tsp salt
1 tsp black pepper
2 large tomatoes, chopped

Place the lentils, chick-peas, potatoes, pumpkin, aubergine, fenugreek, radish, coriander leaves, chillies, mint, turmeric, salt and pepper in a heavy-bottomed pan and cover with water to about 5 cm/2 inches above the surface. Bring to the boil, then reduce the heat and simmer for about 15 minutes, stirring from time to time to prevent sticking. Depending on the size of the pan, you may need to add a little more water. Add the tomatoes and continue cooking for a further 15 minutes, adding a little water if necessary to keep the mixture fairly moist. Test that the lentils are cooked by mashing some of the mixture between your thumb and forefinger or against the side of the pan with a wooden spoon. When cooked, mash the mixture in the pan and set aside.

———————

4 cm/1^1/$_2$ inches roughly chopped ginger
3 cloves roughly chopped garlic
2 tbsp ghee

1 finely chopped onion
500 g/1 lb cubed lamb
1 tsp salt
4 cups water or meat or vegetable stock

Add a little water to the ginger and garlic, blend to a paste and set aside.

Heat the ghee in another heavy-bottomed pan and fry the onion with the ginger and garlic paste until the onion starts to change colour. Add the lamb and salt and fry to seal, then pour in water or stock and simmer for approximately 1 hour. When the lamb is tender, add the mashed vegetables. Stir well, return to the heat and simmer.

2 tbsp ghee
1 finely sliced onion
3 finely chopped red chillies
5 cm/2 inches roughly ground cinnamon stick
2 tsp roughly ground cumin seeds
1 tsp garam masala
¹/₂ tsp saffron threads, steeped for 15 minutes in
1 tbsp hot milk
1 cup water if required

Add the ghee to another pan and fry the onion until it starts to change colour. Add the chillies, cinnamon and cumin seeds and continue frying for 2 minutes, then stir into the meat mixture. Sprinkle in the garam masala and the saffron threads and milk, adding the stock or water if you prefer a moister sauce. Simmer, while continuing to stir, for 3 minutes.

LAMB CUTLETS IN A SPICY TOMATO SAUCE

Khatta Mitha Cutlets

Minced lamb cutlets or patties are slipped into a colourful sweet and sour sauce. Don't be deterred by the number of ingredients – this is a delicious dish and very popular at Parsi weddings. You may wish to serve the cutlets as a starter with one of the breads.

500 g/1 lb finely minced lean lamb
1 large potato, boiled and mashed
2 finely chopped onions
6 cloves finely chopped garlic
4 cm/1¹/₂ inches finely chopped ginger
¹/₂ cup finely chopped coriander leaves
1 tbsp finely chopped mint leaves
4 finely chopped green chillies
1 tsp turmeric powder
1 tsp cumin powder
1 tsp coriander powder
1¹/₂ tsp salt
1 tbsp chick-pea flour
1 lightly beaten egg

Place the mince in a mixing bowl and knead the mashed potato, onion, garlic, ginger, coriander leaves, mint leaves, chillies, turmeric, cumin, coriander, salt, chick-pea flour and beaten egg into the meat. When the mixture is well combined, set it aside and refrigerate for 1 hour or longer so that it becomes firm.

1¹/2 *cups semolina*
2–3 lightly beaten eggs
Ghee or oil for deep-frying

Moisten your hands and form 8 meatballs, flattening them slightly to form cutlets or patties. Then roll in semolina to coat them and dip in the beaten egg. Meanwhile, heat the ghee or oil and deep-fry the cutlets for about 3 minutes or until they turn brown and are cooked through. The cutlets should be kept warm.

---

500 g/1 lb chopped tomatoes
1 tsp cinnamon powder
1 tsp clove powder
¹/2 tsp cardamom powder
4 dried red chillies, crushed
1 tsp salt
250 g/¹/2 lb cooked beetroot, chopped and mashed
3 tbsp malt vinegar
2 tbsp soft brown sugar

Place the tomatoes, cinnamon, clove, cardamom, chillies and salt in a heavy-bottomed pan and bring to the boil, reduce the heat and simmer for about 4 minutes, stirring occasionally to prevent sticking. Remove from the heat, mash the mixture and strain through a fine sieve into a bowl, pressing the solids against the sieve to extract as much liquid as possible. Stir the mashed beetroot into the tomato sauce, return the mixture to the heat, add the vinegar and the sugar and simmer gently.

---

1 tsp oil
2 cloves finely chopped garlic
4 cm/1¹/2 inches finely chopped ginger

While the sauce is simmering, heat the oil in a small pan and fry the garlic and ginger for about 1 minute and then add to the simmering sauce. Slip the cutlets into the sauce and heat through.

PORK CURRY WITH VEGETABLES

Dooker Na Gosht Ni Curry

Although pork is not forbidden to the Parsis, there are very few pork recipes that are specifically Parsi. This is an aromatic curry given a sweet and sour flavour by sugar and tamarind. Cinnamon, cloves and cardamom bring fragrance to the dish, which is made hot with chilli powder and cracked pepper. The pork should contain some fat, which may be drained off before serving if so desired. Potatoes are traditionally included, and carrots may also be added to the dish. Serve with plain rice.

---

4 tbsp vegetable oil
2 finely chopped onions
4 cm/1¹/2 inches finely chopped ginger
6 cloves finely chopped garlic
12 curry leaves
2 cinnamon sticks
6 cloves

Heat the oil in a heavy-bottomed pan. Fry the onions until they start to change colour and then add the ginger, garlic, curry leaves, cinnamon and cloves. Fry for about 2 minutes, adding a little water if the mixture is inclined to stick.

1 tsp cardamom powder
2 tsp cracked pepper
2 tsp chilli powder
2 tsp coriander powder
1 tsp cumin powder
1 tsp turmeric powder
1 tsp mustard powder

Add the cardamom, pepper, chilli, coriander, cumin, turmeric and mustard and stir-fry for 2 minutes, again adding a little water if necessary to prevent sticking.

---

1 kg/2 lb cubed pork, with fat
Salt to taste
1¹/₂ litres/2¹/₂ pints water

Add the cubed pork and salt to the spice mixture and fry to seal. Pour in the water and bring to the boil. Keep the liquid on the boil for about 20 minutes, after which the sauce should be reduced by half.

---

2 large potatoes, cubed
3 large tomatoes, puréed
4 tbsp tamarind pulp steeped for 15 minutes in
1 cup hot water then pushed through a sieve to extract
¹/₂ cup of tamarind liquid
1 tbsp soft brown sugar

Add the potato and cook gently for 1 hour.

Add the puréed tomatoes, tamarind liquid and sugar and simmer for 30 minutes. Test for tenderness. The sauce should be fairly thick.

CHICKEN DISHES

IN INDIA A CHICKEN FOR THE POT is normally bought, alive and fully-feathered, on the day it is to be cooked. In the markets chickens are kept in coops or baskets, and are sometimes strung together. Buying a bird can be a lengthy procedure – first of all, the eyes and the comb (if it is a cock bird) are inspected. Then the chicken is prodded and poked and the breast squeezed for plumpness. Sometimes the poultry-seller will be asked to slit the throat, but in a household where there are servants it is usual for one of them to prepare the bird and hand it over to the cook. In our home in southern India we had two chicken pens. One was for the egg-laying hens and the other for the birds being reared for the table. My sister and I never reconciled ourselves to the throat-slitting procedure, but we were always happy to help with the plucking of the birds.

Chicken is considered by most Indians to be something of a luxury rather than the everyday fare that it has become in the

West. In most recipes, but not quite all, the skin is removed in order to allow the flavours of the spices and marinades to penetrate the meat more thoroughly; most butchers will do this if asked. In supermarkets the job is often done before the chicken pieces are packaged for display. Some people prefer to leave on the skin as it adds more flavour to the sauce, although it also gives it a slightly oily texture.

Chicken always occupies an important place on the menu at Parsi wedding banquets, and I have included two dishes that make regular appearances at such occasions (p.55 and p.57). In both cases, the chicken is marinated in a spiced paste and later deep-fried. They taste quite different, however, one being sweet and sour as a result of the use of Worcestershire sauce, a popular flavouring agent with its spicy tamarind tang, while the other is made tart by marinating the chicken in vinegar and spices before deep-frying.

CHICKEN AND VEGETABLES IN A TANGY SAUCE

Murghi Baffat

If you can, use thick pot-set yoghurt for this dish and, if possible, line a colander with cheesecloth or muslin and drain the yoghurt for a few hours or overnight – you will be surprised at the amount of whey that will drain off. Meat of your choice may be substituted for the chicken.

2 roughly chopped onions
6 tbsp desiccated coconut
6 cloves garlic
30 g/1 oz cashews
3 roughly chopped green chillies
2.5 cm/1 inch cinnamon, broken into pieces
10 cloves
2 tsp cumin powder
3/4 cup thick pot-set yoghurt

Blend the onions, coconut, garlic, cashews, chilli, cinnamon, cloves and cumin powder to a paste in a food-processor.
Stir the blended paste into the yoghurt and set aside.

---

2 tbsp ghee
1 tbsp vegetable oil
2 tsp cumin seeds
2.5 cm/1 inch finely chopped ginger
1 tsp turmeric powder
1 tsp chilli powder
1 large carrot, diced
3 medium potatoes, diced

Heat the ghee and oil together in a heavy-bottomed pan. Add the cumin seeds and ginger and stir-fry for 1 minute. Add the turmeric and chilli powder along with the blended paste and continue cooking until the oil begins to separate out from the spice mixture. Add the carrot and potatoes and cook for a further 5 minutes.

6–8 skinned chicken pieces

Add the chicken pieces, reduce the heat and simmer for approximately 40 minutes until the chicken is cooked and tender.
Serve with a dal and one of the breads.

CHICKEN WITH PINEAPPLE

Ananus Ma Murghi

In India, this sweet and hot dish is usually prepared with a fresh pineapple, the juice of which is also used in the sauce. It is well worth using a fresh pineapple if you possibly can – and remember to retain about half a cup of juice before proceeding with the recipe. The pineapple, originally from the New World, was introduced into India in the mid-sixteenth century and was widely grown by the time Jahangir assumed the Moghul throne in the early seventeenth century.

---

*A medium-sized fresh pineapple or
450 g/16 oz canned pineapple rings*

Top and tail the fresh pineapple, remove the skin and cut into chunks, discarding the core, which is normally tough and fibrous, and saving the juice. If you are using canned pineapple, drain the fruit into a bowl and reserve the juice. Cut the pineapple rings into chunks and set aside.

---

*4 cloves garlic
5 cm/2 inches roughly chopped ginger
1 tsp cumin seeds
4 dried red chillies
1¹/₂ tsp salt
2 tbsp lime or lemon juice
6–8 skinned chicken pieces*

Blend the garlic, ginger, cumin seeds, chilli, salt and lime or lemon juice to a paste. Rub the paste over the chicken pieces and set aside for 1 hour.

———————

6 tbsp vegetable oil or ghee
2 finely chopped onions
8 cloves
5 cm/2 inches cinnamon stick
1 tsp cardamom seeds
2 finely chopped green chillies
1½ cups water

Heat the oil or ghee in a heavy-bottomed pan and fry the onions until they start to change colour. Remove with a slotted spoon to a plate, allowing as much oil as possible to drain back into the pan.

Bring the same oil to a high heat, add the cloves, cinnamon, cardamom and chillies and fry for a few seconds. Add and brown the chicken pieces – you may need to add a little more oil. Then add the water, reduce the heat, cover and simmer for about 10 minutes or until the chicken is almost cooked.

———————

3 tbsp sugar
2 tbsp pineapple juice
¼ cup water
¼ cup pineapple juice

While the chicken is cooking, stir the sugar into the 2 table-spoons of pineapple juice in a small pan and cook on a medium heat until the sugar dissolves and turns an even brown colour.

Coat the pineapple pieces with the caramelised sugar. Add the water and the rest of the pineapple juice and simmer for about 5 minutes to soften the fruit.

Add the pineapple pieces and their juice to the chicken pieces, stir gently to mix and simmer for 5 minutes.

¹/₂ cup cream, pouring consistency

Remove the pan from the heat and gradually add the cream. Mix well and warm through, taking care that the sauce does not boil. If desired, discard the cinnamon stick before serving.

MINCED CHICKEN CUTLETS

Murghi Cutlets

These lightly spiced cutlets or patties of minced chicken will soon become a favourite. You may wish to omit or reduce the quantity of chilli if serving them to children, although in India, of course, most children are introduced to chilli in their food from a very young age.

750 g / 1¹/₂ lb skinned chicken breast, minced
2 cloves finely chopped garlic
2.5 cm / 1 inch grated ginger
3 tbsp finely chopped coriander leaves
2 finely chopped green chillies
2 slices bread, crusts removed, crumbed
2 tbsp plain flour
¹/₂ tsp cumin powder
¹/₂ tsp cumin seeds
1 beaten egg
Salt to taste

Add the garlic, ginger, coriander, chilli, breadcrumbs, flour, cumin powder, cumin seeds, egg and salt to the minced chicken.

Knead well to combine. Moisten your fingers and form into 8 egg-shaped portions, flatten to oval shapes and refrigerate for a couple of hours so that the patties become firm.

---

250 g/8 oz breadcrumbs
Vegetable oil for shallow-frying
2 beaten eggs

Spread the toasted breadcrumbs on a board or platter and press the cutlets into the breadcrumbs to coat all over.

Heat the oil in a frying pan. Dip the cutlets into the beaten egg and shallow-fry, turning gently, for about 5 minutes on each side until a golden colour. Remove and drain on absorbent paper.

SPICY CHICKEN IN TOMATO SAUCE

Tamatar – Ma Murghi

This flavoursome but mildly spiced dish can be prepared quickly and easily. It would make a good introduction to Parsi food for chilli-fearing friends. You may, of course, add more chilli powder if you wish. Finely chopped onions are added in two stages – initially, they are fried with spices as part of the masala as a base to take the chicken pieces, and later with the puréed tomatoes to create the sauce tinged with flavours of cinnamon and clove. Serve with plain rice or a bread.

750 g/1¹/2 lb skinned chicken thigh fillets
3 tbsp vegetable oil or ghee
2 finely sliced onions
2 cloves finely chopped garlic
8 cm/3 inches grated ginger
2 tsp coriander powder
1¹/2 tsp cumin powder
1 tsp chilli powder
¹/2 tsp turmeric powder

Cut the chicken into pieces measuring roughly 5 cm/2 inches. Set aside.

Heat the oil or ghee in a heavy-bottomed pan. Fry the onion until it starts to change colour, then add the garlic and ginger and continue frying for 1 minute. Add the coriander, cumin, chilli and turmeric and cook for 1 minute. If the mixture begins to stick, add a little water and scrape across the bottom of the pan.

Add the chicken pieces, stir to coat and cook until the chicken pieces are sealed.

---

4 large ripe tomatoes, puréed
1 finely chopped onion
3 tbsp finely chopped coriander leaves
1 cinnamon stick
6 cloves
Salt to taste

Add the puréed tomatoes, onion, coriander leaves, cinnamon stick, cloves and salt to the chicken mixture. Bring to the boil, reduce the heat, cover and simmer until the chicken is tender – this should take about 25 minutes. If desired, discard the cinnamon stick before serving.

APRICOT CHICKEN WITH POTATO STRAWS

Sali Jardaloo Ma Murghi

Many Parsi dishes are cooked with both fresh and dried fruits, a tradition that reflects their Persian ancestry. This dish, sweetened with dried apricots and sugar and made sharp with vinegar, is often served at weddings and on festive occasions. The crunchy potato straws called *sali* are traditionally served either piled on top of the chicken or alongside it.

1 kg/2 lb chicken thigh fillets
2.5 cm/1 inch grated ginger
1 clove finely chopped garlic
1 tsp chilli powder
1 tsp cumin powder
1 tsp cardamom powder
1 tbsp vegetable oil

Cut the chicken into large pieces and put into a bowl with the ginger, garlic, chilli, cumin, cardamom and vegetable oil. Rub the oil and flavourings into the chicken pieces and set aside for 1 hour.

2 dried red chillies
5 cm/2 inches cinnamon stick, broken into pieces
1 tsp cumin seeds
1 tsp cardamom seeds
10 cloves
20 dried apricots cut into quarters
2 cups water

Use a coffee-grinder or spice mill to grind coarsely together the chilli, cinnamon, cumin, cardamom and cloves. Set aside.

Put the apricots into a small pan with the water and simmer for 5 minutes. Remove from the heat and leave the apricots to steep until required.

----

6 tbsp vegetable oil
2 finely sliced onions
1 clove finely chopped garlic
2.5 cm / 1 inch grated ginger
2 finely chopped tomatoes
1 cup water
Salt to taste

Heat the oil in a heavy-bottomed pan. Fry the onions, garlic and ginger until the onion starts to become golden. Add the coarsely ground spice mixture, stir and continue frying for 1 minute.

Add the chicken pieces to the onion mixture, together with any juices that have collected and stir-fry for 3 minutes. Add the tomatoes, water and salt. Bring to the boil, reduce the heat, cover and simmer gently for 5 minutes.

2¹/₂ tbsp malt vinegar
1 tbsp sugar

Add the vinegar, sugar and the apricots together with half the liquid in which they have been steeped – discard the remaining liquid. Stir the apricots in with the chicken, cover and continue to simmer for approximately 20 minutes until the chicken is cooked.

----

2 large potatoes, peeled
2 tsp salt
Vegetable oil for deep frying

Cut the potatoes into pieces the size of large matchsticks. Place them in a large bowl, sprinkle with salt, cover with cold water and leave to sit for 15 minutes. Drain, spread the potato straws onto a tea-towel and pat dry, absorbing as much moisture as possible. Heat the oil in a deep pan or fryer. When the oil begins to splutter, add the potato straws in batches and fry until golden and crunchy. Remove with a slotted spoon and drain on absorbent paper.

DEEP-FRIED CHICKEN

Murghi Na Farcha

Chicken pieces coated with spices and then deep-fried feature in a number of Parsi recipes, including this one, which is flavoured with cardamom and cloves. Deep slashes are made in the meat and a spicy paste is then rubbed into the cuts and all over the chicken. The chicken pieces need to be marinated for 4–6 hours, or overnight, whichever is more convenient, after which they are brushed with yoghurt and then deep-fried. Use chicken pieces of your choice. Serve with one of the lentil or vegetable dishes and plain rice, together with a raita.

5 cm/2 inches cinnamon stick, broken into pieces
1 tsp cardamom seeds
16 cloves
1 tsp fennel seeds
1 tbsp coriander powder
4 red chillies

2.5 cm/1 inch grated ginger
1 clove finely chopped garlic
1¹/₂ tsp salt
2 tbsp malt vinegar
2 tbsp water

Blend the cinnamon, cardamom, cloves, fennel, coriander, chillies, ginger, garlic, salt, vinegar and water to a paste.

---

8 chicken pieces, skin removed

Make a couple of deep slashes across each piece of chicken with a sharp knife. Insert a little of the spice paste into the slits and rub the paste all over the meat. Allow to marinate for 4–6 hours or covered overnight in the refrigerator.

---

1 cup lightly whisked yoghurt
Ghee or vegetable oil for deep-frying

Brush the chicken pieces with yoghurt immediately before deep-frying them.

Heat the ghee or oil in a pan deep enough to take the chicken pieces and deep-fry the pieces a couple at a time.

FRIED CHICKEN

Murghi Farcha

This is another popular dish on wedding menus. Chicken pieces are first coated in an aromatic paste that is given a tangy flavour with Worcestershire Sauce and then dipped in an egg batter and deep-fried. If the chicken is cut into bite-sized pieces they may be served with drinks.

750 g/1¹/2 lb chicken breasts, skinned and boned
3 tbsp lime or lemon juice
1 tsp salt

Cut the chicken breasts in half lengthwise and prick in several places. Mix the salt into the lime or lemon juice and rub into the meat. Set aside.

2.5 cm/1 inch roughly chopped ginger
2 cloves garlic
3 roughly chopped green chillies
1 tsp cumin powder
1 tsp turmeric powder
1 tsp cardamom powder
¹/2 tsp cinnamon powder
4 cloves
1¹/2 tbsp Worcestershire Sauce
2 tsp malt vinegar
1 tbsp vegetable oil
¹/2 tsp salt

Blend the ginger, garlic, chillies, cumin turmeric, cardamom, cinnamon, cloves, Worcestershire Sauce, vinegar, oil and salt to a paste in a food-processor. Coat the chicken pieces well with the blended paste, lay on a flat platter, cover and refrigerate for four hours or overnight.

Vegetable oil or ghee for deep-frying
4 well beaten eggs

Heat the oil or ghee in a heavy-bottomed pan. Dip the chicken pieces in egg and deep-fry.

OFFAL

OFFAL HAS GREAT NUTRITIONAL VALUE and used to form an important part of the diet throughout the Western world, but in many countries increased prosperity and changes in fashion have combined to turn it into a minority taste. Fortunately, offal remains standard fare throughout Asia, and it continues to occupy a significant place in Parsi cookery, with liver being the favourite ingredient.

Generally speaking, offal such as lambs' liver and kidneys should be cooked fairly quickly to seal in the juices and leave the centre moist and soft-textured. However the most elaborate dish in this chapter, Minced Lamb with Liver (p.62), is a casserole-type dish that requires lengthy cooking, unlike most liver dishes, where the inside is left slightly pink. Here the finely cubed liver is well cooked and has a firm texture.

Some Western readers may not think that Spiced Chicken

Livers and Gizzard (p.64) sounds very appealing, but for Parsis this is a very special dish, traditionally served as the last of the main courses at wedding banquets. Gizzards, in spite of lengthy cooking time, remain fairly firm-textured, and in this recipe they are parboiled before being added to the spice mixture for further cooking.

I have included a recipe involving brains (p.67), even though they may no longer be bought in the United Kingdom. Brains are a good source of Vitamins A and B and are regarded as a very sustaining food. I have no hesitation in recommending that you cook them in countries where they pose no risk to health.

LAMBS' TONGUES AND LENTILS

Masoor Ma Jeebh

The soft texture and delicate flavour of tongue marries well with the spicy lentils to create a rich and satisfying sauce. The lambs' tongues require lengthy cooking, taking between 1½ and 2 hours. I usually poach them in a light stock with the addition of some white wine. The poaching liquid should simmer very gently – if the liquid is allowed to boil, the tongues will toughen. A skewer should stick through the tongues very easily when they are cooked and tender.

6 lambs' tongues, cooked

Skin the cooked tongues while still warm, then cut in half lengthwise and set aside.

3 tbsp vegetable oil
2 finely sliced onions
2 cloves finely chopped garlic
4 cm/1¹/₂ inches finely chopped ginger
3 large green chillies, slit from base to stem
1 tsp turmeric powder
1 tsp cracked black pepper
2 tsp coriander powder
2 tsp cumin powder
1 tsp salt
2 cups water
250 g/8 oz/1 cup masoor lentils, picked over for grit,
washed and drained
Large pinch asafoetida
3 additional cups water

Heat the oil in a heavy-bottomed pan. Fry the onion, garlic and
ginger until the onion begins to change colour. Add the chillies,
turmeric, pepper, coriander, cumin, salt and the halved tongues
and 2 cups of water. Bring to the boil, then reduce the heat and
simmer for 5 minutes. Add the lentils and asafoetida and stir in
well. Pour the additional water over the mixture and stir. Bring
to the boil, lower the heat and allow to simmer. Cover the pan
and continue cooking on a low heat for about 15 minutes.
Check the contents from time to time and add a little boiling
water if the mixture begins to stick or becomes too dry. Remove
to a serving dish and garnish with fried onion.

---

2 tbsp vegetable oil
1 finely sliced large onion

Heat the oil and fry the sliced onion until it is brown but not
burnt.

MINCED LAMB WITH LIVER

Oombaryoun

This dish is traditionally cooked in an earthenware vessel, broad at the base and narrowing at the neck. The earthenware pot is immersed in water for a couple of hours and the inside then smeared with oil and lined with mango or banana leaves. The pot is covered and sealed with a ribbon of dough before cooking.

This is a simplified version of Oombaryoun. Some recipes call for up to 30 ingredients, including quail and partridge. In this version minced lamb is combined with calf's or lamb's liver. Small flat beans called *sem phali* or field beans are usually used for this recipe in India. They may not be available elsewhere and I have substituted french beans. A casserole dish large enough to take the layered ingredients will be required. It is important for the ingredients to cook in the steam contained within the cooking vessel. This is achieved by sealing the cover to the pot with a ribbon of dough, known in Moghul cooking as the dum method. The quantity of dough needed will depend on the size of your casserole.

500 g / 1 lb french beans
250 g / 1/2 lb finely cubed lamb's or calf's liver
1 tbsp ajwain seeds
2.5 cm / 1 inch grated ginger
1 clove finely chopped garlic
1 tsp turmeric powder
1 tsp cracked black pepper
1 tsp chilli powder

1/2 tsp salt
3 tbsp vegetable oil or 2 tbsp ghee

Top, tail and cut the beans into 2.5 cm/1 inch pieces. Mix the beans with the liver, the ajwain, ginger, garlic, turmeric, cracked pepper, chilli powder, salt and vegetable oil or ghee. Mix well and set aside.

---

500 g/1 lb minced lean lamb
1.5 cm/1/2 inch grated ginger
1 clove finely chopped garlic
1 tsp cracked black pepper
1 tsp turmeric powder
3 tbsp finely chopped coriander leaves
3 finely chopped green chillies
1 beaten egg yolk

Add the ginger, garlic, pepper, turmeric, coriander leaves, chillies and the beaten egg yolk to the mince, mix well to combine. Set aside in the refrigerator to firm.

---

2 small sweet potatoes, unpeeled
3 potatoes, unpeeled
Salt to taste

Wash both varieties of potato, but do not peel them; cut into quarters and mix together. Place alternate layers of potato with the liver and bean mixture into a casserole-type dish with a close-fitting lid. When the layers are complete, sprinkle with salt.

Moisten your fingers and form small meatballs from the mince mixture and place them on top of the final layer in the casserole. Cover and seal the lid to the dish with a ribbon of dough. Place in an oven pre-heated to 180°C/350°F/gas mark 4 and cook for 1 hour. Switch off the oven and leave the dish in it for a further 20 minutes. Remove the seal. The Oombaryoun may be eaten hot or cold, served with chilli, mint and coriander chutney, and washed down with copious quantities of toddy or beer.

SPICED CHICKEN LIVERS AND GIZZARDS

Alaitee Palaitee

Parsis are fond of seasoning their dishes with Worcestershire Sauce. The recipe for this sauce is said to have evolved from one given to two chemists, a Mr Lea and a Mr Perrins, of Worcester in 1823 by an erstwhile Governor of Bengal, so perhaps it is not altogether inappropriate that this sauce, still manufactured in the English Midlands, should feature prominently in Parsi cooking. This dish can be supplemented with the addition of chicken hearts and kidneys. Gizzards require lengthy cooking, but this can be reduced, as in this recipe, by par-boiling them first. Use the resulting stock to add to the spice mixture at the end of the cooking process.

250 g/8 oz chicken gizzards
250 g/8 oz chicken livers

Wash the gizzards and cut them into 6 pieces. Place in a heavy-bottomed saucepan with sufficient water to leave one cup of stock after boiling, and simmer for 20 minutes. Remove the pieces from the pan and set aside, reserving the stock.

Cut each liver into 3 pieces. Set aside.

3 tbsp ghee or vegetable oil
2 finely sliced large onions
2 cloves finely chopped garlic
2.5 cm/1 inch finely chopped ginger
1/2 cup water
1 tbsp finely chopped coriander leaves
1/2 tsp turmeric powder
1 tsp chilli powder
1 tsp garam masala
2 tsp Worcestershire Sauce
Salt to taste

Heat the ghee or vegetable oil in a heavy-bottomed pan and fry the onions, garlic and ginger until the onion becomes light brown in colour. Add the water and simmer for 2 minutes, then the coriander leaves, turmeric, chilli, garam masala, Worcestershire Sauce and salt, and simmer for 3 minutes, adding a little water if the mixture is inclined to stick.

---

1 cup gizzard stock
2 tbsp lime or lemon juice

Add the gizzards and their stock and simmer for 20 minutes. Add the chicken livers and simmer for a further 20 minutes, adding a little water if necessary to keep the mixture moist. On nearing completion, add the lime or lemon juice and simmer for a couple more minutes.

SPICED LAMB'S LIVER

Masala Ni Kaleji

Parsis, like many other peoples, consider liver to be both a delicacy and a giver of strength. When purchasing a whole liver, it ought to be covered with a membrane, which helps keep the meat moist and should be removed only at the time of preparing the liver for the pan. If you intend to cook it immediately after purchase, your butcher will probably remove the membrane and clean the liver for you. In Indian and other Asian cuisines liver is cooked through until there is no sign of blood and there are no vestiges of a pinkish colour. If you prefer, the liver may be diced rather than cut into thin slices. However you choose to prepare the liver, this dish is delicious eaten on buttered toast.

1 lamb's liver
1 tsp salt
1 tsp ground black pepper

Wash the liver and cut it into thin slices. Sprinkle with salt and pepper and set aside.

5 cm/2 inches roughly chopped ginger
6 cloves garlic
2 roughly chopped green chillies
2 tsp cumin powder
2 tbsp lime or lemon juice
2 tbsp vegetable oil

Blend the ginger, garlic, chilli, cumin and lime or lemon juice to a paste and marinate the sliced liver in the mixture for 1 hour.

Heat the oil in a frying pan, add the liver, the marinade and any juices that have been collected and cook to seal. Reduce the heat, cover the pan and simmer gently for 3–4 minutes or until cooked through. Do not over-cook, or the liver will have a tough, leathery texture.

SAVOURY BRAINS

Khara Bheja

Quartered brain is lightly sealed in a masala mixture and then poached in a tomato purée. Vinegar serves as a seasoning in many Parsi dishes, and the most commonly used is that made from sugarcane and dates and fermented with toddy. Do buy Navsari or Valsad vinegar (named after the two cities in India famous for their vinegars) if you are fortunate enough to find them – in this and other recipes I have substituted malt vinegar to give the required acidic flavour.

It is no longer legal to buy brain in Britain, but it is still sold elsewhere in Europe as well as in North America and Australia, and it's well worth making this typically Parsi dish anywhere that the principal ingredient is safe to eat and is to be found in butchers' shops.

4 sheep's brains
2 tbsp malt vinegar

Soak the brains in cold water for 1 hour and then remove all the surrounding membranes. Rinse, pat dry and cut each into 4 pieces. Place the brains in a saucepan, cover them with water, add the vinegar and simmer for 15 minutes. Remove and set aside.

3 tbsp ghee
2 finely sliced onions
5cm/2 inches grated ginger
4 cloves finely chopped garlic
1 tsp turmeric powder
3 finely chopped green chillies
3 tbsp finely chopped coriander leaves
Salt to taste
3 large tomatoes, pureéd

Heat the ghee in a heavy-bottomed pan and fry the onion, ginger and garlic until the onion starts to change colour. Add the turmeric, chilli, coriander leaves and salt and continue frying for 2 minutes. Add the brain and fry on each side to seal. Finally, add the tomatoes and simmer for about 5 minutes.

FISH AND SHELLFISH

IN INDIA IT IS VERY RARE to come across a fish that has simply been fried, grilled or baked. Before cooking, the fish will always be rubbed with salt and turmeric and then sprinkled with lime or lemon juice. It may be coated with spices and chick-pea flour, or stuffed with grated coconut and fresh coriander and mint.

Parsi cooking often combines fish with lentils. The pulses are either served as an accompaniment spooned over plain cooked rice or prepared as a sauce to take the fish, and the combination of fish and lentils makes for a rich and satisfying meal.

The Indian coastline is thousands of miles long and its waters yield an immense variety of fish and shellfish, while their freshwater cousins breed in the country's vast rivers, countless streams, lakes, ponds and rice paddies. It is little wonder that the Chinese traveller Xuan Zang, who spent over sixteen years travelling in India in the seventh century AD, expressed his amazement at the many species of fish available.

It is not easy to relate species of fish found in Indian waters to those caught around Britain or North America, and matters are made more confusing by the many regional languages spoken in India. Comparisons have, however, been made between the fish caught in the North Atlantic and those found in the Indian Ocean. Dover sole has been likened to pomfret, shad to hisla, halibut to seer and cod to sangara. In the recipes that follow, I simply suggest firm white-fleshed fish, leaving the choice subject to availability. An exception are the recipes that call for Bombay Duck, which is famously not a duck but a salted dried fish (p.88 and p.89).

I have often visited one of Bombay's smaller suburban markets with a Parsi friend who normally has fish for his midday meal. In the fish section rows of women sat side by side with baskets gleaming with the catch brought in by their menfolk earlier that day. They knew him well and he had his favourite stallholders for different types of fish, but he never bargained with them, which I thought was rather unusual. He explained to me that bargaining is expected in India, but that as a very regular customer a system of trust had built up between him and his carefully selected fish-sellers. Not so, I noted, with other shoppers – the fishermen's wives drove a very hard bargain, interspersed with a lot of laughter as they chided their customers for trying to beat them down in price.

BAKED FISH WRAPPED IN BANANA LEAVES

Kena Na Patta Ma Bhoojeli Machhli

Banana leaves are widely available in Asia, Africa and elsewhere, and they provide a cheap natural casing in which to seal and cook a variety of ingredients. The leaves are blanched and then cut down the middle to remove the thick central vein. Kitchen foil makes a good substitute for banana leaves where these are not available. Cut the foil pieces sufficiently large to encase and seal the pieces of fish. Traditionally, palm sugar is the sweetening agent used in this recipe, but because it is not easily available outside the subcontinent I have substituted soft brown sugar. Do use palm sugar if you can, as it lends a distinctive treacly flavour to the fish.

750 g/1¹/₂ lb firm white fish fillets
1 tsp salt

Cut the fish into large pieces, wash and pat dry. Sprinkle with salt and set aside.

6 cloves garlic
4 roughly chopped fresh green chillies
1 cup roughly chopped coriander leaves
60 g/2 oz desiccated coconut
3 tbsp lime or lemon juice
1 tbsp tamarind concentrate
2 tbsp soft brown sugar

2 tsp dry-roasted cumin seeds
1 tsp salt

Blend the garlic, chillies, coriander leaves, coconut, lime or lemon juice, tamarind, sugar, cumin and salt to a paste. Smear the paste over the pieces of fish and allow to marinate for 1 hour.

---

2 tbsp ghee

Grease the pieces of foil liberally with ghee, place a piece of fish in the centre of a piece of foil and fold over the edges to seal the fish completely. Smear an oven-proof dish with ghee, place the wrapped pieces of fish in the dish and put into an oven pre-heated to 180°C/350°F/gas mark 4 and cook for 30 minutes. Unwrap one of the parcels to check whether the fish is cooked through. The cooking time will vary depending on the thickness of the fish fillets.

STEAMED FISH COATED IN CHUTNEY

Patra Ni Machhi

Fish pieces are coated in a paste of coriander, mint leaves and chillies. Traditionally they are wrapped and cooked in banana leaves, which are sometimes available from oriental stores and have been used in Asian cooking for centuries. Kitchen foil cut into squares makes an acceptable substitute if banana leaves are not available. Cut the foil into squares large enough to wrap each piece of fish separately.

500 g/1 lb thick, firm white fish fillets
1 tsp salt

Cut the fillets into individual serving sizes, sprinkle with salt and set aside.

———————

8 tbsp desiccated coconut
1 cup roughly chopped coriander leaves
1/4 cup roughly chopped mint leaves
4 roughly chopped green chillies
1 tsp cumin seeds
6 cloves garlic
2 tsp sugar
1 tsp salt
2 tbsp lime or lemon juice
1 tbsp ghee for greasing

Pre-heat the oven to 180°C/350°F/gas mark 4. Blend the coconut, coriander leaves, mint, chillies, cumin seeds, garlic, sugar, salt and lime or lemon juice to a paste. Rub the paste over the fish pieces. Wrap and seal each piece of fish in a greased square of foil. Place the fish on a metal rack in a baking tray with enough hot water to cover the base while leaving the rack clear. Steam in the pre-heated oven for 20 minutes or until the fish is cooked through.

Serve individually, allowing your guests to unwrap the parcels themselves.

FISH WITH BASIL AND POMEGRANATE SEEDS

Tulsi Aur Anardana Macchi

Pomegranate seeds add an unexpected flavour and a crunchy bite to this dish in which the fish is first rubbed with a garlic and ginger marinade, then lightly fried and served with a tomato-based sauce infused with flavours of basil leaves and fresh coriander.

3 large red chillies
6 cloves garlic
5 cm/2 inches ginger
2 tbsp lime or lemon juice
1 tsp turmeric powder
4–6 firm white fish fillets

Blend the chilli, garlic, ginger and lime or lemon juice to a paste and then mix in the turmeric powder. Coat the fish fillets with the paste and set aside for 30 minutes.

Flour for coating
3 tbsp vegetable oil

Heat the oil in a heavy-bottomed frying pan. Sieve the flour lightly over the fish fillets and fry them on both sides for 2–3 minutes, depending on thickness, until golden. Remove to a serving dish, cover with foil and keep warm, reserving the remaining oil.

1 tbsp vegetable oil
4 cm/1½ inches grated ginger
2 tsp finely chopped garlic
2 tsp dry-roasted cumin seeds
3 tbsp pomegranate seeds
3 large tomatoes, chopped
2 tbsp finely chopped basil leaves
2 tbsp finely chopped coriander leaves
Salt to taste

If necessary, add 1 tablespoon of oil to the oil remaining from the previous stage and heat. Add the ginger, garlic, cumin and pomegranate seeds and stir-fry for 1 minute. Then add the tomatoes, basil, coriander leaves and salt and simmer gently for 2 minutes. Pour over the fish fillets and serve immediately.

COCONUT-FLAVOURED FISH WITH AUBERGINE

Patio Taji Machhli No

This hot, spicy dish goes well with puréed lentils and plain rice and a chutney or pickle. Aubergine is a very versatile vegetable and can be cooked in a variety of ways – fried, grilled, braised or baked. Here it is stewed with spices, tamarind and coconut milk and will take on their flavours as well as that of the fish. Tamarind concentrate is available from oriental food stores. If you prefer to use fresh tamarind, follow the instructions on p.32.

500 g/1 lb aubergine cut into cubes
1 tsp salt
6 cloves garlic
4 green chillies
1/2 cup coriander leaves
1 tsp cumin seeds
2 tbsp lime or lemon juice
1 tbsp soft brown sugar
1 tbsp tamarind concentrate
1 cup boiling water

Sprinkle the salt over the cubes of aubergine. Set aside and allow to sweat.

Blend the garlic, chillies, coriander leaves, cumin seeds and lime or lemon juice to a paste and set aside.

Dissolve the sugar and the tamarind concentrate in the boiling water and set aside.

---

1 tbsp ghee
2 tbsp oil
2 finely chopped medium onions
1 tbsp chick-pea flour
1 tsp turmeric powder
1 tsp coriander powder
1 tsp cumin powder
11/2 cups water
1 tsp salt
11/2 cups canned coconut milk

Heat the ghee and the oil together in a heavy-bottomed pan and fry the chopped onions until the colour begins to change. Then add the blended paste, chick-pea flour, turmeric, coriander and cumin and continue frying for 2 minutes. Add a little water and scrape across the bottom of the pan if the mixture is inclined to stick. Stir in the cubed aubergine, the water and salt, and simmer for about 10 minutes or until the aubergine softens. Add the tamarind extract and simmer for 2 minutes. Remove the pan from the heat and gradually add the coconut milk. Return to the heat and bring the sauce to the boil.

---

500 g/1 lb firm white fish fillets, cut into large pieces
4 large tomatoes, cut into quarters

Add the fish pieces and tomatoes to the sauce and simmer for about 8 minutes or until the fish is cooked through. This will depend on the thickness of the pieces. When the fish turns opaque and is white and firm, it should be cooked through.

PRAWNS IN A NUTTY SAUCE

Colmi No Patio

The nutty flavour in this sauce comes from almonds, poppy and sesame seeds ground into a paste with spices and coconut, while the bite comes from dried chillies and peppercorns. The souring agent traditionally used to make this dish is a type of plum called *cocum*, which can sometimes be found in oriental (especially Gujarati) stores; if it is unavailable, substitute lime or lemon juice. If you use pre-cooked prawns to make this dish, simply add and heat them through just before serving.

---

500 g/1 lb medium-sized raw prawns

Shell the prawns and devein them by cutting a shallow slit along the outer curve and lifting or scraping out the gritty vein. Rinse the prawns lightly and set aside.

6 dried red chillies
6 cloves garlic
1¹/₂ tsp cumin seeds
10 blanched almonds
2 tsp poppy seeds
2 tsp sesame seeds
12 peppercorns
6 cloves
60 g/2 oz freshly grated or desiccated coconut, moistened
with a little water
4 tbsp lime or lemon juice
3 tbsp water

Blend the chillies, garlic, cumin, almonds, poppy seeds, sesame seeds, peppercorns, cloves, coconut, lime or lemon juice and the water together into a paste and set aside.

3 tbsp ghee or vegetable oil
2 finely chopped onions
3 large tomatoes, chopped
1¹/₂ cups canned coconut milk

Heat the ghee or oil in a heavy-bottomed pan and fry the chopped onion until the colour starts to change, then stir in the blended paste and the chopped tomatoes and cook for 3 minutes. Add the coconut milk and simmer on a low heat until the oil begins to separate out. Add the prawns and cook for about 3 minutes or until they change colour.

PRAWNS WITH OKRA

Bhinda Colmi No Patio

Okra is indigenous to Africa, but nowadays is so widely grown in the subcontinent that India is said to be the world's largest producer of this nutritious vegetable, which is rich in fibre, vitamins and folic acid. If you use pre-cooked prawns to make this sweet and sour dish, simply heat them through just before serving. Serve with one of the breads and a chutney.

250 g / 1/2 lb raw prawns
1 tbsp lime or lemon juice

Shell and devein the prawns following the instructions in the previous recipe. Rinse, pat dry and dribble with lime or lemon juice. Set aside.

250 g / 1/2 lb okra
Sesame oil for deep-frying
1 clove garlic
4 roughly chopped green chillies
1/2 cup coriander leaves
1 tbsp cumin seeds
1 tbsp malt vinegar
1 tsp turmeric powder

Wash the okra, cut and discard the stem ends and slice into 2.5 cm/ 1 inch pieces. Heat the oil and deep-fry the okra pieces for 1 or 2 minutes until they become slightly crispy, but are still green in colour. Remove and drain on kitchen paper, retaining the remaining oil.

Then blend the garlic, chillies, coriander and cumin seeds with the vinegar to a smooth paste. Add the turmeric to the paste, mix well and set aside.

-----

4 tbsp sesame oil retained from deep-frying
2 finely chopped onions
3 large tomatoes, finely chopped
2 tsp soft brown sugar
2 tsp chilli powder
Salt to taste

Heat the oil in a heavy-bottomed pan and fry the onion until it starts to change colour. Add the blended paste and stir-fry for 2 minutes. Add the chopped tomato, sugar, chilli powder and salt, reduce the heat and allow the mixture to simmer for 2 minutes.

Add the prawns and okra and simmer gently until the prawns turn pink and are cooked.

FISH COOKED IN YOGHURT AND SPICES

Machhi No Callo

The sauce in this piquant dish combines the flavours and textures of nuts, spices, chillies and garlic ground together to make a smooth sauce with yoghurt, which is made yet more aromatic with fresh coriander leaves and steeped saffron threads before the fish fillets are introduced. You might think that all these flavours would overpower the fish, but do try it –

you will be pleasantly surprised.

-----

500 g/1 lb firm white fish fillets
2 tsp salt
2 tbsp lime or lemon juice

Cut the fish into 4 pieces, wash them and pat dry with kitchen paper. Sprinkle with salt and lime or lemon juice. Set aside.

-----

30 g/1 oz blanched, slivered and toasted almonds
30 g/1 oz blanched, chopped and toasted pistachios
³/4 cup freshly grated or desiccated coconut
¹/2 cup hot water
1 tsp dry-roasted cumin seeds
2.5 cm/1 inch dry-roasted cinnamon stick
1 tsp dry-roasted cardamom seeds
3 roughly chopped red chillies
2 roughly chopped green chillies
4 cloves garlic

Blend the almonds, pistachios, coconut, water, cumin seeds, cinnamon, cardamom, chillies and garlic to a paste. Set aside.

-----

¹/2 cup yoghurt
1 tbsp dry-roasted sesame seeds

Add the sesame seeds to the yoghurt and set aside for 15 minutes.

-----

3 tbsp ghee
2 finely chopped onions
1 green chilli, slit lengthwise
1 cup chopped coriander leaves

125 g/4 oz fresh green peas
1/2 tsp saffron threads steeped in
1 tbsp warm milk for 15 minutes

Heat the ghee in a heavy-bottomed saucepan and fry the chopped onions until they turn golden brown. Stir in the paste mixture and fry for about 3 minutes or until the ghee begins to separate out, add the chilli, coriander leaves, yoghurt and sesame seeds and bring to the boil.

Reduce the heat, place the fish fillets in the sauce, add the peas and the saffron threads in milk and simmer for 10–15 minutes until the fish is cooked through. Remove to a serving platter and scatter potato straws from the final stage of the recipe over the surface.

2 tbsp ghee
1 large potato, cut into pieces the size of large matchsticks

Fry the potato straws until crisp and golden. Remove with a slotted spoon and dry on absorbent paper.

FISH WITH PIGEON PEAS

Dhan Dhar Ne Machhi No Patio

This is another dish that is often served at Parsi wedding feasts. The large yellow pigeon peas known as *toovar* or *arhar* are not spiced, while the fish is cooked in a fairly dry sauce made with a heady combination of cloves, chillies, cumin and cinnamon. Rinse the pigeon peas well and allow time for them to soak for

4 hours or overnight. Begin by cooking the pigeon peas first and then gently re-heating them as and when required.

---

3 dried red chillies
3 tbsp malt vinegar
2.5 cm/1 inch cinnamon stick, broken into pieces
15 cloves
1 tbsp cumin powder
1 roughly chopped onion
1/2 tsp salt

Break the chillies into the vinegar in a non-metallic bowl and set aside for 10 minutes.

Add the chillies and vinegar to the cinnamon, cloves, cumin, onion and salt, blend to a rough paste and set aside.

---

3 tbsp vegetable oil
2 finely chopped onions
4 tbsp water
750 g/1 1/2 lb firm white fish fillets

Heat the oil in a heavy-bottomed pan and fry the onion to a light brown colour. Add the paste and stir-fry until the oil starts to separate out, gradually adding the water to prevent sticking.

Cut the fish into 5 cm/2 inch pieces, add them to the spice and onion mixture and simmer until the fish is cooked through.

---

400 g/14 oz toovar (pigeon peas)
Salt to taste
1 tsp turmeric powder

Drain the pigeon peas and cover well with water, add the salt and turmeric and cook until the dal can be mashed. More water may be required during cooking to obtain a thick soup texture.

Mash the dal when soft. Set aside and reheat if necessary.

---

2 tbsp vegetable oil
5 cloves finely chopped garlic

Heat the oil in a small pan, fry the garlic until it starts to change colour; immediately pour over the mashed dal and mix well. Then spoon the pigeon peas over plain white rice and serve with the fish.

SPICY FISH WITH LENTILS

Dhan Dhar Ne Machhi No Patio

Although this recipe bears the same name in Gujarati as the previous one, and both combine fish with a lentil sauce, there are significant differences in both the ingredients and the method and so in the resulting flavours. This is really a dish of two recipes; one is a lentil stew flavoured with garlic, onion and a pinch of turmeric and cumin. This is spooned over plain white rice and accompanied by fish or prawns in a thick spicy sauce. It is served on auspicious occasions. You can start to prepare the fish dish and to brown the onions for the garnish while the lentils are cooking. The lentils may be gently re-heated just before serving.

---

5 cups water
250 g/¹/₄ lb masoor (small orange) lentils
¹/₂ tsp turmeric powder
1 tsp salt

Wash and drain the lentils and put them into a heavy-bottomed pan with water, turmeric and salt and cook for about 15 minutes or until the lentils are mushy and easily mashed. The texture should be that of a thick soup.

2 tbsp ghee
1 tsp cumin seeds
1 finely chopped small onion
6 cloves finely chopped garlic
6 dried red chillies
2 roughly chopped onions
2 tbsp malt vinegar

Heat the ghee in a small pan. Add the cumin seeds, onion and garlic, stir-fry over a high heat for 2 minutes and pour over the dal. Set aside whilst preparing the fish and re-heat if necessary immediately before serving.

Blend the chillies, onions and vinegar into a paste and set aside.

500 g/1 lb firm white fish fillets
1 tsp salt
1 tsp turmeric powder
3 cloves garlic
1 tbsp cumin powder

Cut the fish into large pieces, wash and pat dry. Sprinkle the fish with salt and turmeric. Crush the garlic into the cumin powder and rub onto the fish pieces. Set aside.

3 tbsp ghee
3 chopped tomatoes
Salt to taste
2 tsp sugar

2 tbsp malt vinegar
¹/₂ cup finely chopped coriander leaves

Heat the ghee in a heavy-bottomed pan and fry the chilli and onion paste until it starts to darken in colour. Add the chopped tomatoes and salt, reduce the heat and stir and simmer for 2 minutes. Add the sugar and vinegar, bring to the boil and add the fish pieces together with any juices that may have collected. Reduce the heat and simmer for about 10 minutes or until the fish is almost cooked. Stir in the coriander leaves and complete the cooking. Remove to a serving dish.

---

3 tbsp ghee
3 finely sliced onions

Heat the ghee and fry the onion until brown in colour. Remove with a slotted spoon and scatter over the fish.

SWEET AND SOUR FISH

Sas Lagansara

This is another auspicious dish that is often served at wedding feasts. One version calls for double the quantity of chillies given here – if your guests' palates and stomachs are not averse to intense heat, you may wish to add more chillies.

---

750 g/1¹/₂ lb firm white fish fillets
1 tbsp salt
1 tbsp flour

Combine the salt and flour, rub into the fish and set aside.

---

2 tbsp ghee
2 finely chopped onions
12 curry leaves
3 cloves garlic
10 green chillies
2 cups water or fish stock
12 finely chopped small tomatoes

Heat the ghee and fry the onion and curry leaves until the onion starts to change colour.

Blend the garlic and chillies to a paste and add to the onion mixture. Stir-fry for about 2 minutes and then add the water or stock together with the tomatoes. Bring to the boil, then reduce the heat, add the fish and simmer until the fish begins to turn opaque. Remove from the heat and set aside.

---

1 cup malt vinegar
3 tbsp sugar
100 g/3$^{1}/2$ oz rice flour
2 tsp finely chopped mint leaves
2 tbsp finely chopped coriander leaves
1 tbsp cumin
$^{1}/2$ cup water
6 lightly beaten eggs

Beat the eggs lightly in a bowl and add the vinegar, sugar, rice flour, mint, coriander, cumin, water and tomatoes. Return the fish mixture to a gentle heat, add the egg mixture and simmer for about 2 minutes, taking care not to allow the sauce to boil, or it will curdle.

BOMBAY DUCK PATTIES

Boomla Na Cutlass

The pungent smell of Bombay Duck being cooked can be offensive to some people, rather like the durian fruit which is claimed 'to smell like hell but taste like heaven'.

If the mixture doesn't hold together well when forming into patties, add a little of the beaten egg and about 1 tablespoon of flour to the mixture.

---

25 Bombay Ducks

Cover the Bombay Ducks with water and soak them overnight. Drain, remove the central bones and blend to a rough paste in a food-processor. Set aside.

---

3 tbsp ghee
2 finely chopped onions

Heat the ghee in a heavy-bottomed pan and fry the onion to a light golden colour. Add the onions to the Bombay Duck paste and set aside.

---

1 tsp cumin seeds
1 tsp cumin powder
1 tbsp soft brown sugar
$1/2$ tsp cracked black pepper
2 roughly chopped green chillies
$1/2$ cup chopped coriander leaves
2 cloves garlic

2.5 cm/1 inch finely chopped ginger
1 tsp tamarind concentrate, dissolved in
2 tbsp hot water
Salt to taste

Blend the cumin seeds, cumin powder, sugar, pepper, chillies, coriander leaves, garlic, ginger and tamarind juice together in a food-processor. Mix this masala into the Bombay Duck and onion mixture and refrigerate for a couple of hours to firm up.

---

2 beaten eggs
250 g/8 oz breadcrumbs
Vegetable oil or ghee for shallow-frying

Form the mixture into small patties, dip them in the beaten egg and coat with breadcrumbs.

Heat the oil or ghee in a large frying pan and shallow-fry the patties for about 2 minutes on each side, turning once.

SPICED AND PICKLED BOMBAY DUCK

Tarapori Boomla No Patio

Vinegar acts as a preservative in this pickle-like dish made with salted dried fish, which is said to come from the town of Tarapore. The original recipe called for 9 red chillies in addition to 3 teaspoons of chilli powder, which resulted in a very fiery concoction, and even though I have reduced the quantities it is still quite powerful. Serve as an accompaniment to any of the fish dishes or as a sandwich filling.

---

30 Bombay Ducks

Wash and pat dry the fish, then cut them into small pieces, cover with water and set aside for 15 minutes.

---

2 roughly chopped onions
2 cloves garlic
2.5 cm/1 inch ginger
2.5 cm/1 inch cinnamon stick broken into small pieces
4 cloves
5 roughly chopped red chillies
1 tbsp soft brown sugar
2 tbsp malt vinegar

Blend the onion, garlic, ginger, cinnamon, cloves, chillies, sugar and vinegar to a paste.

---

4 tbsp sesame oil
2 tsp turmeric powder
2 tsp chilli powder
1 tbsp dry-roasted and ground coriander seeds
1 tbsp dry-roasted and ground cumin seeds
1 cup malt vinegar
Salt to taste

Drain the fish and place it in a heavy-bottomed pan, stirring in the blended paste, sesame oil, turmeric, chilli powder, coriander, cumin, vinegar and salt. Cook on a gentle heat for about 10 minutes, stirring occasionally until the oil starts to separate out and the fish is cooked.

EGG DISHES

EGGS ARE A SYMBOL OF FERTILITY AND LIFE in many cultures and religions, and they play a significant part in Parsi rituals. At weddings, eggs are placed on a tray together with rice, coconut and fresh flowers. A pre-nuptial ceremony is performed by a senior lady of the household, usually the mother of the bride, who will take an egg in her right hand and rotate it seven times over the groom's head. The egg is then smashed next to the groom's feet. The number seven, often incorporated into ritual, is held to be very auspicious. The rotating of the egg is supposed to infuse energy into the celebrant and it is believed that if there is any evil destined towards the groom it will be absorbed by the egg, the smashing of which ensures the destruction of the evil. Egg dishes always appear on the menu at Parsi weddings, at which Eggs with Onion and Coriander (p.94) is a great favourite, and which would be considered incomplete without the rich Wedding Custard (p.150).

Eggs are rich in iron and vitamins A and B as well as a useful source of protein. Eggs are economical and, when combined with ingredients such as vegetables, they make a substantial and nourishing meal.

As a child growing up in India the daily appearance of the egg vendor was always an event I looked forward to. The egg-man would arrive each morning carrying cane baskets suspended at each end of a bamboo pole. With great dexterity, he would swing the pole forward and place the covered baskets on the ground. I would sit alongside the cook and watch the ritual of testing the eggs for freshness by placing them in a bowl of water. The eggs should lie flat on their sides at the bottom of the bowl – if an egg stands vertically or floats to the surface it is an indication of staleness. I would squeal with delight and quickly pick the stale eggs out of the bowl and hand them back to the egg-man – he promptly put them back into the basket and would try to sell them to his next customer.

BAKED EGGS WITH SPICY BANANAS

Kera Per Eeda

Cooking eggs with bananas may seem slightly eccentric to Western eyes, but the combination is a rich and tasty one and is a favourite with egg-eating vegetarians. Use large, ripe firm bananas for this dish. When sliced, sprinkle the banana with lime or lemon juice to prevent discolouring. If the bananas are sliced too thinly, they will tend to break up.

6 ripe firm bananas
1 tbsp lime or lemon juice

Peel and slice the bananas into rings ½ cm/¼ inch thick. Sprinkle with lime or lemon juice and set aside.

---

2 tbsp ghee or vegetable oil
3 finely sliced onions
2 cloves finely chopped garlic
2.5 cm/1 inch finely chopped ginger
½ tsp turmeric powder
2 finely chopped green chillies
3 tbsp finely chopped coriander leaves
1 finely chopped large tomato
Salt to taste
4–6 eggs

Heat the ghee or oil in a large heavy-bottomed pan. Fry the onion, garlic and ginger until the onion starts to change colour. Stir in the turmeric, chilli, coriander, tomato and salt and stir-fry for 2 minutes. Add the slices of banana and mix in gently. Meanwhile, pre-heat the oven to 180°C/350°F/gas mark 4.

Spread the mixture evenly into a baking dish. Make depressions with the back of a spoon and break each egg into a depression. Cover with foil and bake for approximately 15 minutes or until the eggs are done to your liking.

EGGS WITH ONION AND CORIANDER

Cothmir Per Eeda

A typical Parsi way of cooking eggs is to break them onto a bed of a savoury and spicy mixture. The main ingredient for the bed could be mince, tomatoes, spinach, potato or dried fish, combined with an onion-based masala. This particular dish is often served at Parsi wedding banquets.

2 tbsp vegetable oil
4 finely diced onions
¹/2 tsp cumin seeds
2.5 cm/1 inch grated ginger
4 cloves finely chopped garlic
2 finely chopped green chillies
¹/2 tsp turmeric powder
1¹/2 cups finely chopped coriander leaves
Salt to taste
4–6 eggs

Heat the oil in a heavy-bottomed frying pan and fry the onion until golden. Then add the cumin seeds, ginger, garlic, chillies, turmeric, coriander leaves and salt and continue to stir-fry for 3 minutes. Spread the mixture into a baking dish. Break the eggs on top of the mixture. Cover with a lid and simmer on a gentle heat for about 3 minutes or until the eggs are set to your liking.

OMELETTE WITH GINGER AND CORIANDER

Masala No Poro

If you have a large frying pan, the egg mixture may be cooked in one slab and then cut into serving-size portions. There are various versions of this recipe – in this one the ingredients are blended to a paste, but they may also be finely chopped and added to the beaten egg. This spicy dish is often accompanied by a jam or sweet chutney.

1 roughly chopped onion
1/2 cup chopped coriander leaves
2 roughly chopped green chillies
2.5 cm/1 inch ginger
2 cloves garlic
1/2 tsp turmeric powder
2 tbsp lime or lemon juice
Salt to taste

Blend the onion, coriander, chillies, ginger, garlic, turmeric, lime or lemon juice and salt to a paste. Set aside.

6 eggs
1 finely chopped large tomato
1 tbsp oil

Beat the eggs to a froth and add them to the blended paste together with the chopped tomato and stir to mix. Heat the oil, preferably in a non-stick frying pan, and pour the egg mixture into the hot oil. Cook the mixture until the underside is set firm and golden in colour. Flip over and cook the other side until golden brown. Serve immediately.

SAVOURY SCRAMBLED EGGS

Akoori Eedani

There are many variations to the typical Parsi breakfast dish of scrambled eggs. A moister texture can be obtained with the addition of a little milk or cream to the beaten egg. The dish can be made even tastier with the addition of 2 tablespoons of finely chopped green garlic stem or chopped chives. The dish is then called *Akoori Leela Lasanni* or green garlic-flavoured scrambled eggs.

2–3 tbsp ghee or butter
1 medium onion, finely chopped
4 cm/1¹/₂ inches finely chopped ginger
2 small potatoes, cut into tiny cubes
2 finely chopped green chillies
1 cup chopped coriander leaves
1 medium tomato, finely chopped
1 tsp cracked pepper
¹/₂ tsp salt
4 whisked eggs

Heat the ghee or butter in a heavy-bottomed pan and sauté the onions and ginger with the cubed potato until the onions begin to change colour and the potatoes are cooked. Add the chilli, coriander leaves, tomato, pepper and salt and cook for a further 2 minutes.

Reduce the heat and add the beaten eggs. Stir the mixture until the egg is set and serve immediately.

SPICY HARD-BOILED EGGS

Akoori Bafelan Eedan Ni

This simple but tasty dish is quick and easy to prepare. It can be made more substantial with the addition of peas or any finely diced vegetable. It can also be turned into a non-vegetarian dish by adding minced lamb or beef to the potatoes at the frying stage.

4 eggs

Hard-boil the eggs, shell and cut them into 3 horizontal slices. Arrange the egg slices in a shallow dish and set aside.

3 tbsp ghee
2 finely chopped onions
4 cm/1½ inches finely chopped ginger
2 finely cubed potatoes
2 finely chopped green chillies
1 cup finely chopped coriander leaves
2 tbsp finely chopped mint leaves

1 tbsp Worcestershire sauce
Salt to taste

Heat the ghee and fry the onion, ginger and potato together until the potato is cooked. Then add the chillies, coriander and mint and fry until softened. Add the Worcestershire Sauce and salt. Spread the mixture over the eggs and serve with one of the breads and a chutney.

SPICY SCRAMBLED EGGS

Lasan-Marchan Na Charvelan Eedan

Most Parsis are very fond of egg dishes and there are numerous variations on the theme of spicy scrambled eggs – each family, of course, claims its version to be the most delicious of all. The quantities given here will provide 6 generous servings. Remember to remove the mixture from the heat before it becomes dry – the texture should be rich and creamy. The eggs can be made even more flavoursome with the addition of chopped prawns.

3 tbsp butter
1 finely chopped onion
2 cloves finely chopped garlic
1.5 cm/¹/2 inch finely chopped ginger
1 finely chopped green chilli
1 small firm ripe tomato, chopped
¹/2 tsp salt
2 tbsp finely chopped coriander leaves

Heat the butter, add the onion, garlic and ginger and fry until the onion becomes translucent. Add the chilli, tomato and salt and continue cooking for 1 minute, then stir in the chopped coriander. Remove from the heat while preparing the eggs.

8 eggs

Beat the eggs and add them to the onion and ginger mixture, lower the heat and cook gently. Remove from the heat while the mixture is soft and creamy – it will continue to cook off the heat. Serve with buttered toast.

BAKED EGGS WITH SPICY VEGETABLES

Tarkari Per Eedan

Whisked eggs are poured or spread over a spicy mixture of cooked potatoes and turnips and then baked in the oven. The egg yolks and whites can be whisked separately if a lighter texture is preferred. Although the method calls for the vegetables to be stir-fried, I usually speed up the cooking process by par-boiling the potatoes and turnips beforehand. This makes a good supper dish served with hot buttered toast.

3 tbsp ghee
2 finely sliced onions
2 finely sliced potatoes

2 finely sliced turnips

Heat the ghee in a heavy-bottomed pan and fry the onions, potatoes, and turnips until they are almost cooked.

———————

1 large puréed tomato
3 finely chopped green chillies
2.5 cm/1 inch finely chopped ginger
4 cloves finely chopped garlic
1 cup chopped coriander leaves
1 tsp turmeric
$^1/_2$ cup water
1$^1/_2$ tsp salt
4 whisked eggs
4 whole spring onions, cut into rings

Add the tomato, chillies, ginger, garlic, coriander leaves, turmeric, water and salt to the vegetable mixture and simmer for about 5 minutes until the vegetables are cooked. Meanwhile, pre-heat the oven to 180°C/350°F/gas mark 4. Spoon and spread the mixture into an oven-proof dish, pour the whisked eggs over the top and bake for about 15 minutes or until the egg mixture is set.

Remove from the oven, divide into serving portions and serve immediately with a generous sprinkling of sliced spring onion.

SPICED OMELETTE

Eedan No Poro

Flavoured with onion, chilli, coriander and tomato and lightly spiced with pepper, turmeric and cumin, this omelette can be prepared in next to no time. This recipe is an invaluable standby if friends drop by unexpectedly – you will be able to have a light but nutritious meal on the table in a matter of minutes. The quantities given here are for two people.

3 lightly beaten eggs
1 finely chopped onion
2–3 finely chopped green chillies
2 tbsp finely chopped coriander leaves
1 medium tomato, finely chopped
1/2 tsp ground black pepper
1/4 tsp turmeric powder
1/2 tsp cumin powder
Salt to taste
3 tsp ghee

Mix all the ingredients together in a small bowl.

Heat the ghee in a small non-stick frying pan, pour in the egg mixture and fry on one side. Turn when the underside becomes light brown and fry and set the other side.

BAKED EGGS WITH TOMATOES

Tomato Per Eeda

Whole eggs are slipped into a sweet and sour tomato base and baked in the oven until set. I often serve this for brunch or supper with hot buttered toast.

1¹/₂ tsp vegetable oil
2 finely sliced large onions
1 tsp cumin seeds
3 cloves finely chopped garlic
2 finely chopped green chillies
3 tbsp finely chopped coriander leaves
Salt to taste
4 large ripe tomatoes, chopped
1 tsp sugar
1 tbsp malt vinegar
4–6 eggs

Heat the oil in a heavy-bottomed pan, fry the onions and the cumin seeds until the onion starts to change colour. Add the garlic, chilli, coriander leaves, salt, tomatoes, sugar and vinegar, reduce the heat and simmer for 3 minutes. Spread the mixture evenly into a baking dish. Make depressions into the mixture with the back of a spoon. Break an egg into each depression and bake in an oven pre-heated to 180°C/350°F/gas mark 4 until the eggs are set. Serve immediately.

VEGETABLES AND PULSES

VISITING OUTDOOR FRUIT AND VEGETABLE MARKETS is one of the great pleasures of a visit to India. Markets are always a multicoloured bustle of activity, packed with people noisily selecting and bargaining for the freshest produce available, and the enormous variety of vegetables is a photographer's delight. The camera, however, can only capture the visual spectacle, and there is no substitute for the aromatic impact of actually strolling past the displays piled high with bright green coriander, shiny red and green chillies, creamy garlic, large mounds of plump, fresh ginger and white and purple aubergines.

As a result of the air-freighting of fruit and vegetables around the world, nearly all the produce on offer in an Indian market can be found today in markets, shops and supermarkets in Birmingham, Chicago and Sydney. There is a growing debate about the wisdom of flying fruit and vegetables around the planet, but there is no denying that the kitchens and dining-tables of northern Europe and North America have been transformed beyond recognition by the availability of fresh peppers, aubergines, ginger and other produce throughout the year, even though this has led to the obliteration of the seasons. Melons and strawberries are no longer treats to be looked forward to in high summer, but are to be found on supermarket shelves when there is snow on the ground outside. Okra and mangoes – never seen fresh outside tropical or sub-tropical regions a generation ago – are now as easily found as onions and apples in Manchester or Boston. The environmental cost of flying foodstuffs from one hemisphere to another is considerable and 'food miles' are the subject of sometimes impassioned debate, but there is no doubt that our culinary horizons have expanded massively with the easy availability of what were once rare and exotic ingredients. Lovers of the cooking of the Indian subcontinent in northern climes have been amongst the principal beneficiaries of this revolution in food transport.

YAM CUTLETS

Suran Na Cutlace

The use of hard cheese in this dish is a clear indication of colonial influence, as most Indian cheeses are soft-textured rather than hard and cured like Western ones. To avoid waste and mess, place the patties and the egg mixture next to the pan before dipping and frying them. Serve with Tangy Salad (p.175) and Lime and Date Chutney (p.177).

This recipe works equally well by replacing yam with mashed potato.

---

500 g/1lb yam
2 finely chopped onions
2 tbsp grated hard cheese
10 finely chopped mint leaves
1 1/2 cups finely chopped coriander leaves
1 clove finely chopped garlic
1.5 cm/1/2 inch finely chopped ginger
2–3 finely chopped green chillies
1/2 tsp turmeric powder
1/2 tsp cracked black pepper
Salt to taste
1 beaten egg yolk – reserve the white
2 tbsp cornflour

Peel, boil and mash the yam. Add the onion, cheese, mint and coriander leaves, garlic, ginger, chillies, turmeric, pepper and salt into the mashed yam. Mix in the egg yolk and the cornflour.

---

250 g/8 oz breadcrumbs
2 eggs and reserved egg white, beaten
Ghee or vegetable oil for shallow-frying

Form the mixture into patties or cutlets and coat all over with breadcrumbs. Beat the eggs with the egg white reserved from the previous stage, dip the patties into the egg mixture and shallow-fry in hot oil or ghee for about 2 minutes on each side until golden. The egg will frill around the patties as they fry.

SWEET AND SOUR PUMPKIN

Lal Koru

There are numerous varieties of pumpkins, which come in many shapes, sizes and colours. In this recipe the pumpkin is peeled, but if you prefer to use butternut pumpkin or another variety with an edible skin you will need to allow extra cooking time. Pumpkin skins can be hard to peel, so use a sharp knife. If you buy pumpkin by the piece, rather than whole, make sure to select a moist- rather than a dry-looking chunk. You will need to scrape and remove the stringy fibres and the seeds when preparing the pumpkin for the pan.

2 roughly chopped green chillies
1/2 cup coriander leaves
5 cm/2 inches roughly chopped ginger
4 cloves garlic
2 tbsp water

Blend the chillies, coriander, ginger, garlic and water to a smooth paste and set aside.

2 tbsp ghee
2 finely chopped onions
1 tsp chilli powder
2 tsp cumin powder
2 tsp coriander powder
1 kg/2 lb peeled and diced red or yellow pumpkin

Heat the ghee in a heavy-bottomed pan and fry the onions until they start to change colour, then add the chilli, cumin and coriander and fry for 1 minute. Add the blended paste and stir-fry for 2 minutes, stirring in a little water if the mixture is inclined to stick.

Add the diced pumpkin and mix well to coat.

---

1 tbsp soft brown sugar
2 tsp tamarind concentrate
1 cup hot water
Salt to taste
1 tbsp lime or lemon juice

Dissolve the sugar and the tamarind concentrate in hot water and pour over the pumpkin mixture. Add the salt and lime or lemon juice and simmer for about 20 minutes until the pumpkin is soft. Serve with one of the rice dishes and a pickle.

SPICY AUBERGINE AND TOMATO

Kacha Tambota Me Vengna

The first stage of this recipe involves searing, but not burning, the skin of an aubergine over an open flame – the skin will darken and wrinkle and begin to peel away in places, giving the flesh a rich, smoky flavour. If you can't cook over an open flame, a similar effect can be achieved by pre-heating the oven to its maximum temperature, placing the aubergine on a rack and turning it until the skin really wrinkles and darkens. Timing will vary depending on the size of the aubergine. Pushing a long skewer through the aubergine will help considerably with the turning. This makes a delicious accompaniment to any of the rice dishes and also goes well with Prawns in a Nutty Sauce (p.77).

---

1 or 2 large aubergines with a total weight about 500 g/1 lb
3 tbsp ghee or vegetable oil

Push a long skewer through the aubergines and smear a little of the ghee or oil on them. Sear the skins over an open flame, turning frequently until the skin wrinkles and begins to peel. When cool, remove the skin and mash the flesh. Set aside.

---

1 finely chopped large onion
3 finely chopped green chillies
6 cloves finely chopped garlic
5 cm/2 inches finely chopped ginger
2 tsp dry-roasted cumin seeds
1 tsp turmeric powder
1 tsp coriander powder
2 tsp garam masala
2 tsp brown sugar
1 tsp cracked black pepper
2 tbsp finely chopped fresh coriander
1 tbsp finely chopped mint
3 finely chopped large tomatoes
Salt to taste

Heat the remaining ghee or oil in a heavy-bottomed pan and fry the onion, chilli, garlic and ginger until the onion starts to change colour. Add the cumin seeds and fry for a few seconds. Stir in the turmeric, coriander powder, garam masala, sugar and cracked pepper and fry for 2 minutes, adding a little water if the mixture is inclined to stick. Add the fresh coriander, mint, tomatoes and salt and simmer for 2 minutes until the tomatoes are soft and slightly pulpy. Finally, fold in the aubergine flesh, stir and simmer for about 2 minutes.

LIGHTLY SPICED PIGEON PEAS

Dhan Dal

Like most inhabitants of the Indian subcontinent, Parsis are keen eaters of legumes and pulses, or dals, and many Parsi dishes combine various types of dal with meat, chicken or rice. Most dals require soaking for about 4 hours to soften and release some of the starch and to render them more digestible, and also to speed up the cooking time. The water in which the dal has been steeped should always be discarded. These pigeon peas make a good accompaniment to Prawns in a Nutty Sauce (p.77) and plain rice.

250 g/8 oz toovar (pigeon peas)
1 1/2 tsp salt
1 tsp turmeric
Water to cover the dal

Rinse the pigeon peas until the water runs clear. Then cover them with cold water and set aside for 4 hours, or overnight in the refrigerator.

Drain the pigeon peas and place them in a heavy-bottomed pan with the salt and turmeric. Cover with water and bring to the boil. Reduce the heat and simmer until the pigeon peas can be squashed between your finger and thumb or against the side of the pan. More hot water may be needed while cooking the pigeon peas. The resulting mixture should not have a sloppy texture. When cooking is complete, mash the contents and set aside.

2 tbsp ghee
2 finely chopped large green chillies
4 cloves finely chopped garlic
2 tsp cumin seeds
¹/₂ cup chopped coriander leaves

Heat the ghee, toss in the chillies, garlic, cumin seeds and coriander leaves and fry lightly for a few seconds. Add to the pigeon pea mixture and mix well.

LIGHTLY SPICED SWEET POTATOES

Chaas Payelo Sakarand

I must admit that I was slightly sceptical when the renowned Parsi cook Katy Dalal told me that she served this as a breakfast dish. Shortly afterwards I experimented by serving it at brunch with Spiced Omelette (p.101) and realised how wrong I had been to question her culinary wisdom – the two dishes complemented each other perfectly and this has since become one of my favourite recipes.

500 g/1 lb sweet potatoes
1 tsp salt

Boil the sweet potatoes whole and unpeeled in salted water; cooking time will vary according to the size of the potatoes – they are ready when a skewer slips easily through the centre. Allow to cool, then remove their skins and cut into wedges.

375 g/12 oz sugar
³/4 cup water
1 tsp cardamom seeds
1 cinnamon stick
1 tsp vanilla essence
Ghee or vegetable oil for deep-frying

Place the sugar and water in a heavy-bottomed pan with the cardamom and cinnamon and make a sticky but runny syrup. Remove from the heat as it begins to change colour, add the vanilla essence and set aside. Discard the cinnamon stick.

Heat the ghee or vegetable oil and fry the sweet potato wedges until they turn a golden colour. Remove with a slotted spoon and place them in the syrup. Stir gently to coat all the pieces and serve immediately.

SWEET AND SOUR VEGETABLES

Lagansala Estew

This sweet and sour stew of mixed vegetables receives its flavouring from sugar and vinegar and is another popular wedding dish. All the vegetables except the beans should be diced small and similarly-sized. Cut the beans into very short lengths approximately the same size as the diced potato and carrot. Allow sufficient oil for the cubed vegetables to be shallow-fried individually first.

Vegetable oil for shallow-frying

150 g/5 oz cauliflower florets
125 g/4 oz peeled and diced potato
125 g/4 oz peeled and diced carrots
150 g/5 oz peeled and diced sweet potato
125 g/4 oz stringed French beans cut into very short lengths
50 g/2 oz diced green pepper

Stir-fry each of the vegetables separately for about 2 minutes. Remove with a slotted spoon. Mix all the vegetables together in a bowl and set aside.

3 tbsp ghee
3 finely sliced onions
2 cloves finely chopped garlic
2.5 cm/1 inch finely chopped ginger
2 finely chopped green chillies
1/2 cup finely chopped coriander leaves
1/2 tsp turmeric powder
Salt to taste
2 finely chopped tomatoes
3 tbsp malt vinegar
2 tbsp sugar

Heat the ghee in a heavy-bottomed pan and fry the onion, garlic and ginger until the onion starts to change colour. Then add the chilli, coriander, turmeric, salt and tomatoes and simmer for 2 minutes. Stir in the vinegar and sugar. Add the vegetables, mix well and cover the pan and simmer for about 10 minutes until all the vegetables are cooked, stirring from time to time. If the mixture is inclined to stick, add a little water.

AUBERGINE FRITTERS

Vengna Na Cutles

These fritters make a delicious starter or can be served with drinks. Sliced aubergine is first sweated with salt, sprinkled with vinegar and then coated with nuts and spices. When frying the fritters, cook them over a gentle flame, turning several times to ensure they are cooked on the inside. If you are using miniature, finger-size aubergines, remove the stems and cut in half along the length. If using the larger variety, you may wish to slice them lengthwise and then cut across to get half-moon shapes. They may be served immediately or kept warm in an oven on a very low heat.

2 large aubergines with a total weight about 350 g/12 oz
Salt
1 tsp cracked black pepper
2 tbsp malt vinegar

If using the large aubergines, cut the stem away and either slice in circles about $^1/_2$ cm/$^1/_4$ inch thick or cut in half along the length and cut into semi-circles and prick lightly. Sprinkle both sides with salt allowing to sweat for about 3 minutes. Sprinkle with vinegar and set aside.

2 cloves garlic
2.5 cm/1 inch ginger
1 tsp dry-roasted cumin seeds
1 tsp chilli powder
1 tbsp sesame seeds

1 tbsp unsalted cashew nuts
2 tbsp lemon juice

Blend the garlic, ginger, cumin, chilli, sesame and cashew nuts with the lemon juice in a food-processor and smear the resulting paste over the aubergine slices.

---

2 cups breadcrumbs
3 well beaten eggs
Vegetable oil for shallow-frying

Press both sides of the aubergine pieces into the breadcrumbs while heating the oil in a large frying pan. Dip the bread-crumbed slices into the egg mixture and shallow-fry a few slices at a time for about four minutes, turning them frequently to ensure the insides are cooked. The cooking time will depend on the size and thickness of your pan, and you may wish to test a piece first before proceeding with the frying stage. Remove the fritters onto absorbent paper.

RICE DISHES

WHEN VISITING MARKETS IN INDIA I always stop and spend some time at the rice stalls. The rice-seller usually sits on a low wooden platform surrounded by hessian sacks opened to expose pearly white grains of husked and polished rice, because although husked but unpolished brown rice is more nutritious, Indians generally prefer polished white rice. I am always fascinated to watch and listen to housewives as they buy their rice, moving from sack to sack as they finger and smell the grains, even taste-testing the rice. Then come the questions before a purchase is made: 'Where was this rice grown?' – 'When did you buy it?' – 'How long have you been storing it?' If the household can afford to do so, rice will be stored for a year or longer, as aged rice is much preferred. The chemical composition of old and new rice is different and new rice is believed to be less easily digested. Older rice will swell to three times its volume when cooked, whilst newer rice will only expand to twice its original size – an important consideration in poorer households.

In south and central India and some eastern parts of the country short-grain rice is the staple food. It will often be eaten twice a day with two or more curries of vegetables, meat, chicken, fish or pulses. Very poor homes content themselves with rice and pulses, plain yoghurt and a green chilli or two to crunch. In northern India wheat is made into a variety of breads for daily fare, but it is from the north that the classic biryanis and pilaus originated in Moghul times, reflecting the Persian influence on Indian cooking.

The Parsis are very fond of their rice creations, especially kedgerees which combine rice with pulses. This style of cooking rice is said to have been introduced to the Moghul courts by the Parsi priests who attended the Emperor Akbar's religious forums in the sixteenth century. The recipes that follow range from Plain White Rice (p.116) to the aromatic Orange-Flavoured Rice with Dates (p.132) with its subtle mixture of orange zest, raisins, almonds and saffron, and Prawns with Coconut-Flavoured Rice (p.131), which brings together rice and beans with cinnamon, chillies and prawns.

PLAIN WHITE RICE

Bafela Safed Chawal

In most Indian households a special pot is reserved for boiling rice so that the cooked rice is untainted by colour or flavour. Use a cooking vessel large enough to allow the rice to expand.

2 cups/500 g/1 lb basmati rice
12 cups/3 litres/6 pints hot water
2 tsp salt

Pick over the rice for grit and stones, then rinse it until the water runs clear. Cover with water and stand for 20 minutes. Drain and allow to dry.

Bring the water to a rolling boil in a deep pan. Add the drained rice and salt. Bring back to the boil and cook uncovered for 6 minutes. Reduce the heat and, with the cover slightly ajar, cook for a further 6 minutes. To check whether the rice is properly cooked, squeeze a few grains between your thumb and forefinger – the centre should not be hard and chalky. Then drain through a sieve or colander.

CARAMELISED SPICY RICE

Khara Chawal

Basmati is my favourite rice variety – it gives off a beautiful aroma when cooking and has a delicious nutty flavour. This slightly sweet rice is flavoured with cloves, cardamom and cinnamon and given a brownish tinge by the addition of caramelised sugar.

2 cups/500 g/1 lb basmati rice
1 1/2 tbsp sugar
1/2 cup/125 ml/4 fl oz hot water

Pick over the rice for grit and stones, then rinse it until the water runs clear. Cover with water and stand for 20 minutes. Drain and allow to dry.

Add the water to the sugar, simmer over medium heat until the sugar is dissolved and the liquid browned. Set aside.

---

3 tbsp vegetable oil or ghee
3 finely sliced onions
4 cloves
1/2 tsp cardamom seeds
1 tsp cumin seeds
1 cinnamon stick
10 peppercorns
3 1/2 cups/850 ml/1 3/4 pints hot water
Salt

Heat the oil in a heavy-bottomed pan and fry the onion until brown. Remove half the onion with a slotted spoon and set aside. Return the pan to the heat, add the cloves, cardamom, cumin, cinnamon and peppercorns and fry for a few seconds to release their aromas.

Add the rice and fry for 3 minutes. Add the sugary water and mix in well.

Add the hot water and salt to the rice mixture and bring to the boil. Reduce the heat, cover with a close-fitting lid and simmer for 20 minutes. Remove the cover and fork through gently. Place a tea-towel over the pan and cover. Allow to stand for 10 minutes before serving.

PRAWN PILAU

Colmi No Palav

Prawns are first seasoned then cooked with onion and tomato, made aromatic with saffron threads. Rice is cooked separately with a spicy masala, and when done the prawn mixture is gently folded in. Diced and fried potato may be added along with the prawns.

Pre-cooked prawns may be used, in which case omit the seasoning with salt, chilli powder and turmeric, and just heat the prawns gently before adding them to the cooked rice.

---

1 1/2 cups/350 g/12 oz basmati or long-grain rice

Pick over the rice for grit and stones, then rinse it until the water runs clear. Cover with water and stand for 20 minutes. Drain and allow to dry.

---

500 g/1lb shelled and deveined prawns
1 tsp salt
1 tsp chilli powder
1 1/2 tsp turmeric powder
6 cloves garlic
3 green chillies
1 tbsp cumin seeds

Sprinkle the prawns with salt, chilli and the turmeric powder. Set aside.

Blend the garlic, chillies and cumin seeds in a food-processor and set aside.

4 tbsp ghee
3 finely sliced onions
1/2 tsp saffron threads steeped for 15 minutes in
1 tbsp warm milk
1 large tomato, chopped

Heat the ghee in a heavy-bottomed pan and stir-fry the onions until they start to change colour. Remove half the fried onions to a plate and set aside. Stir the seasoned prawns, the steeped saffron threads and the chopped tomato in with the remaining onion and stir-fry for a few minutes or until the prawns change colour and are cooked through. Remove from the heat and set aside.

---

1 tbsp ghee
2.5 cm/1 inch cinnamon stick
10 bruised cloves
8 bruised cardamom pods
15 bruised black peppercorns
1 finely chopped red chilli
10 curry leaves
2 tsp salt
125 g/4 oz shelled green peas
1 large tomato, chopped
3 cups/750 g/1 1/2 pints water

Heat the ghee. Return the reserved fried onion to the pan along with the blended paste. Add the cinnamon, cloves, cardamom, peppercorns, chilli, curry leaves and salt and stir-fry for 3 minutes. Add the rice and stir-fry until the rice becomes translucent. Stir in the shelled peas and the chopped tomato, mixing well. Add the water, bring to the boil, cover the pan with a close-fitting lid, reduce the heat to low and cook for 15–20 minutes. Remove the lid and gently fork through, lifting and loosening the rice. Fold the prawn mixture carefully into the rice. Serve with Green Mango and Pineapple Chutney (p.173).

SPINACH PILAU

Palak Pilau

Spinach is the principal vegetable in this pilau, to which diced potato and carrot add both colour and flavour. The potato and carrot are fried before adding to the dish. Par-cooked rice is layered into a baking dish with the spinach mixture and the fried vegetables and cooked in the oven. To prepare for the layering of rice and vegetable, divide both the cooked spinach mixture and the fried vegetables into two portions and the rice into three portions.

---

2 cups/500 g/1 lb basmati rice

Pick over the rice for grit and stones, then rinse it until the water runs clear. Cover with water and stand for 20 minutes. Drain and allow to dry.

---

3 tbsp vegetable oil
3 finely sliced onions
1/2 tsp turmeric powder
1 tsp chilli powder
1 tbsp Worcestershire Sauce
2 tsp soft brown sugar
Salt to taste
500 g/1 lb finely chopped spinach

Heat the oil in a heavy-bottomed pan. Fry the onion until it is light brown in colour. Remove half the onion with a slotted spoon and set aside. Continue frying the rest of the onion and add the turmeric, chilli powder, Worcestershire Sauce, sugar and salt. Simmer for 2 minutes. Add the spinach and cook to wilt. Divide into 2 portions and set aside.

3 tbsp vegetable oil
2 finely diced potatoes
2 finely diced carrots
3$^1/_2$ cups/850 ml/1$^3/_4$ pints hot water
2 tsp salt
1 cup/250 ml/8 fl oz chicken or meat stock
1 tbsp melted ghee

Heat the oil in a deep pan and fry the potatoes and carrots separately. Remove from the oil with a slotted spoon and set aside. Add the rice to the remaining oil and stir-fry for 2 minutes. Then add the hot water and salt, bring to the boil, reduce the heat, cover and simmer until the moisture is mostly absorbed. This should take 10 minutes. Divide the rice into 3 portions. Layer one portion of rice into a casserole with a lid, spread with spinach mixture, potato and carrot and the reserved onion. Repeat this layer. Dribble the stock and ghee over the final layer of rice. Cover with a close-fitting lid and place for 30 minutes in an oven pre-heated to 180°C/350°F/gas mark 4.

LAMB BIRYANI

Gosht No Palav

This biryani is an explosion of flavours. First, there is the masala blend of onion, garlic, ginger and chillies, followed by aromatic cardamom, cinnamon, nutmeg and mace with a bite from both chilli and peppercorns, while the rice and lamb have both a tangy taste from the yoghurt and a hint of sweetness from the raisins and almonds. Except on very special occasions, this would be a meal in itself served with a bowl of plain yoghurt.

Drain the yoghurt of whey overnight. Pour the yoghurt into a colander lined with muslin or cheesecloth over a bowl, cover and refrigerate. Prepare the garnish as the rice is nearing completion.

1 roughly chopped onion
1 clove roughly chopped garlic
4 cm/1 1/2 inches roughly chopped ginger
4 dried red chillies, broken into pieces
4 tbsp lime or lemon juice

Blend the onion, garlic, ginger, chillies and lime or lemon juice to a smooth paste and set aside.

2 cups/500 g/1 lb basmati rice
2 tsp salt
6 cups/1 1/2 litres/3 pints water

Rinse the rice until the water runs clear. Cover it with water and soak for 15 minutes, then drain and set aside for 30 minutes to dry. Boil the water in a heavy-bottomed pan, stir in the rice and salt and cook for 3 minutes. Drain and set aside.

2 tbsp ghee
1 finely chopped onion
2 tsp light-coloured cumin seeds
1 tsp black cumin seeds
10 bruised cardamom pods
5 cm/2 inches cinnamon stick

20 black peppercorns
10 cloves
1 tsp nutmeg powder
2 tsp mace powder
1 kg/2 lb lean lamb cut into 2.5 cm/1 inch cubes
1 tsp salt
6 cups/1½ litres/3 pints water
1 kg/2 lb yoghurt, drained of whey

Heat the ghee in a heavy-bottomed pan, add the onion and the blended paste and stir-fry until the onion starts to change colour. Add the cumin seeds, cardamom, cinnamon, peppercorns, cloves, nutmeg and mace powder and stir-fry for a few seconds to release their aromas. Then add the cubed lamb and salt and stir-fry to seal. Pour the water over and stir well to mix. Cover and simmer until the liquid evaporates and only about 1 cup remains. Remove from the heat, stir in the yoghurt and set aside.

---

2 tbsp ghee
125 g/4 oz slivered almonds
125 g/4 oz raisins
2 finely diced potatoes

While the meat is cooking, heat the ghee in a small pan and fry the almonds until they are a light golden colour and remove them with a slotted spoon. Add the raisins to the remaining ghee and stir-fry until they begin to puff up and remove with a slotted spoon. Stir-fry the potatoes in the remaining ghee, adding a little more ghee if necessary. Remove with a slotted spoon.

Layer one third of the rice into an oven-proof casserole dish with a close-fitting lid, spread one third of the meat mixture over the rice and dot with almonds, raisins and diced potatoes. Repeat this with two more layers.

1/2 tsp saffron threads, steeped for 15 minutes in
1 tbsp warm milk

Sprinkle the saffron threads and milk over the final layer. Cover the casserole and, to prevent steam from escaping, create a seal with crimped foil and place in an oven pre-heated to 160°C/325°F/gas mark 3 and bake for 30 minutes. Fork through gently and mound onto a serving platter.

---

2 tbsp ghee
30 g/1 oz slivered almonds
60 g/2 oz tbsp raisins
1 finely sliced onion
3 hard-boiled eggs cut into rings

Heat the ghee and toss and fry the almonds to a light golden colour; remove with a slotted spoon. Add the raisins to the remaining ghee and stir-fry until they puff up, then remove with a slotted spoon. Add the onion to the ghee until light brown, sprinkle the nuts, raisins and onion over the mound of rice and decorate the edge of the rice with rings of hard-boiled egg.

RICE WITH BEANS AND LENTILS

Plain Khichdi

This simple dish can be prepared fairly quickly. Unlike many of the pulses and legumes used in Asian cooking, neither the orange-red masoor lentils nor the yellow mung beans need to be soaked before cooking. Serve this plain kedgeree with a sauce-based curry like Spicy Chicken in Tomato Sauce (p.51) or Coconut-Flavoured Fish with Aubergine (p.75).

2 cups/500 g/1 lb basmati rice
1/4 cup/50 g/2 oz masoor lentils
1/4 cup/50 g/2 oz split mung beans

Pick over the rice for grit and stones, then rinse it until the water runs clear. Cover with water and stand for 20 minutes. Drain and allow to dry.

Rinse the pulses until the water runs clear. Cover with water and stand for 15 minutes. Drain.

1 tsp turmeric powder
2 tsp salt
4 1/2 cups/1 1/4 litres/2 1/4 pints hot water

Place the rice and pulses in a pan and mix them together well. Stir in the turmeric powder, salt and hot water and bring to the boil. Reduce the heat, cover with a close-fitting lid and simmer gently for 20 minutes. Remove the cover and fork through gently. If the mixture appears too dry, sprinkle a little hot water over the surface after forking through. Replace the cover and allow to stand for 10 minutes before serving.

LIGHTLY SPICED RICE

Vagharela Chawal

This easily prepared, lightly spiced recipe is an everyday rice dish that makes a tasty alternative to rice steamed by the absorption method or boiled in lots of water and drained. When a light lunch is required, this rice may be served with plain yoghurt. Use either basmati or short-grain rice.

2 cups/500 g/1 lb rice

Pick over the rice for grit and stones, then rinse it until the water runs clear. Cover with water and stand for 20 minutes. Drain and allow to dry.

2 tbsp ghee
2 finely chopped onions
3 cloves finely chopped garlic
2.5 cm/1 inch grated ginger
2 finely chopped green chillies
1 cinnamon stick
8 cloves
1/2 tsp cardamom seeds
2 tsp salt
3 1/2 cups/850 ml/1 3/4 pints hot water or stock

Heat the ghee in a heavy-bottomed pan, add the onion, garlic, ginger, chilli, cinnamon, cloves and cardamom and stir-fry for 3 minutes. Add the rice and fry for a few seconds until the rice takes on a shiny appearance. Then add the salt, hot water or stock, bring to a rapid boil and reduce the heat. Cover and simmer on a low heat for 20 minutes. Remove the cover, lift and fork through gently. Place a tea-towel over the pan, replace the cover and allow to stand for 10 minutes.

YELLOW RICE WITH MUNG BEANS

Bafeli Khichdi

Whole mung beans are small, round and green, although they can split open during cooking to reveal a yellow inside. The beans are sometimes sold with their skins on, or split without their skins. They are rich in potassium, iron and calcium and are easily digested. This mildly spiced dish is particularly suitable for small children.

2 cups/500 g/1 lb basmati rice
1 cup/250 g/8 oz whole green mung beans

Pick over the rice for grit and stones, then rinse it until the water runs clear. Cover with water and stand for 20 minutes. Drain and allow to dry.

Pick the mung beans over for stones or grit. Rinse in several changes of water. Cover with water and stand for 15 minutes. Drain and allow to dry.

3 tbsp ghee
1 tsp cumin seeds

5 cm/2 inches cinnamon stick
6 cloves
1/2 tsp cardamom seeds
1 finely chopped onion
1 tsp turmeric powder
1 tbsp desiccated or grated fresh coconut
2 tsp salt
4 1/2 cups/1 1/4 litres/2 1/4 pints hot water or stock

Heat the ghee in a heavy-bottomed pan. Add the cumin seeds, cinnamon, cloves, cardamom and fry for a few seconds to release their aromas. Add the onion, turmeric, coconut and salt. Stir in the rice and mung beans, then add the water or stock. Bring to the boil, stir to mix, reduce the heat, cover and simmer for 15 minutes. Lift the cover and fork through. Check whether the mixture is becoming too dry and, if necessary, sprinkle a little hot water over the surface. Replace the lid and cook for 5 minutes. Remove from the heat and allow to stand for 5 minutes. Remove the lid and fork through gently.

HOT AND SPICY RICE

Barra Mirchi – Khichdi

Dried chillies give this recipe a bite that is further emphasised with the addition of whole peppercorns. I usually serve this with dishes that are mild in heat content like Lightly-Spiced Lamb Stew (p.30) or Lamb with Apricots (p.33). It goes well, too, with Prawns in a Nutty Sauce (p.77).

3 cups/750 g/1¹/₂ lb basmati rice
18 cups/4¹/₂ litres/9 pints water
2 tsp salt

Pick over the rice for grit and stones, then rinse it until the water runs clear. Cover with water and stand for 20 minutes. Drain and allow to dry.

Bring the water to a rolling boil, add the rice and the salt and boil rapidly for 12 minutes. To check whether the rice is properly cooked, squeeze a few grains between your thumb and forefinger – the centre should not be hard and chalky. Drain and set aside to cool.

---

2 tbsp ghee
2 tsp cumin seeds
4 dried red chillies broken into small pieces
4 cloves finely chopped garlic
10 curry leaves
2.5 cm/1 inch cinnamon stick
10 cloves
10 peppercorns
8 bruised cardamom pods
8 finely chopped whole spring onions
2 green chillies cut into fine strips
Salt to taste
¹/₂ cup/125 ml/4 fl oz vegetable or chicken stock or water

Heat the ghee in a heavy-bottomed pan, add the cumin, dried chilli, garlic, curry leaves, cinnamon, cloves, peppercorns and cardamom and stir-fry for 2 minutes. Add the spring onion and green chilli strips and continue frying for 2–3 minutes. Then add the stock or water, reduce the heat and simmer for 2 minutes. Stir in the cooked rice and heat through.

PRAWNS WITH COCONUT-FLAVOURED RICE

Colmi Sathe Khichdi

In this version of kedgeree rice and mung beans are cooked in coconut milk and the result can be a little sticky, like risotto. The flavours of coconut and prawns mingle with whole spices in a dish with the unmistakable bite of chilli.

2 cups/500 g/1 lb basmati rice
1 cup/250 g/8 oz whole mung beans

Pick over the rice for grit and stones, then rinse it until the water runs clear. Cover with water and stand for 20 minutes. Drain and allow to dry.

Pick over the beans for grit and stones, then rinse them in several changes of water. Cover with water and stand for 15 minutes. Drain.

3 tbsp ghee
2 finely chopped onions
3 finely chopped green chillies
1 cinnamon stick
8 cloves
1/2 tsp cumin seeds
1/2 tsp fennel seeds
1 tsp turmeric powder
2 tsp salt
4 1/2 cups/1 1/4 litres/2 1/4 pints canned coconut milk

Heat the ghee in a heavy-bottomed pan, then stir-fry the onions, chilli, cinnamon, cloves, cumin, fennel and turmeric until the onion starts to change colour. Add the rice, mung beans and salt and fry for 2 minutes. Add the coconut milk and bring to the boil, then reduce the heat and simmer for 5 minutes.

300 g/10 oz shelled and deveined prawns

Rinse the prawns in a colander and stir into the rice mixture. Cover and simmer for 15 minutes. If you are using pre-cooked prawns, add them after 10 minutes of simmering. Remove the cover and fork through the rice. If it seems too dry, sprinkle 1/2 cup of water over the surface and continue cooking for 3 minutes. Place a tea-towel over the pan, replace the cover and allow to stand for 10 minutes.

ORANGE-FLAVOURED RICE WITH DATES

Suntra Khajoor Ni Khichdi

The Persian influence on this elaborate dish is evident in the use of dates, almonds and orange zest. Masoor (orange-red) lentils are among the most easily digested pulses and have the advantage of not needing to be soaked before cooking. You will need to divide up the ingredients as indicated, into 2 or 3 portions, in order to create layers of flavours.

This fruity and aromatic dish goes well with Deep-fried Lamb Kebabs (p.37) and plain yoghurt.

3 cups/750 g/1¹/₂ lb basmati rice
1 cup/250 g/8 oz masoor lentils
3 cups/750 ml/1¹/₂ pints water
¹/₂ tsp turmeric powder

Pick over the rice for grit and stones, then rinse it until the water runs clear. Cover with water and stand for 20 minutes. Drain and allow to dry.

Pick over and rinse the lentils until the froth subsides. Put them into a pan with the water and turmeric, bring to the boil and cook for 10 minutes. Drain, divide into 2 portions and set aside.

———————

2 tbsp ghee
1 finely sliced onion
2 tbsp slivered orange peel
3 tbsp raisins
250 g/8 oz pitted dates, roughly chopped
2 tbsp slivered almonds

Heat the ghee in a non-stick frying pan and fry the onion until it starts to change colour. Then mix in the orange peel, raisins, dates and almonds and stir-fry for 1 minute. Set aside in 3 portions.

———————

8 cups/2 litres/4 pints water
1 tbsp salt

Bring the water to the boil in a heavy-bottomed pan, add the salt and the drained rice to the boiling water and keep on a rolling boil for 10 minutes. Drain, divide into 3 portions and set aside.

———————

¹/₂ cup/125 ml/4 fl oz melted ghee
¹/₂ cup/125 ml/4 fl oz vegetable oil
3 tbsp yoghurt

1 tsp saffron threads steeped for 15 minutes in
2 tbsp warm milk
1 tsp cardamom powder
¹/₂ tsp cumin powder
¹/₂ tsp cinnamon powder
¹/₂ tsp mace powder
1 tsp cracked black pepper

Wipe dry and use the same pan to heat one tablespoon each of the ghee and oil. Reserve the remaining ghee and oil. Spread one portion of the rice into the pan and dribble 1 tablespoon of yoghurt over it. Sprinkle one third of the saffron strands in milk and one portion of the fruit and nut mixture over this layer of rice. Mix the remaining spices together and divide them into 3 portions. Sprinkle one portion of spices over the first layer and then spread over 1 portion of the cooked lentils.

Repeat the next layer as above. The final layer will not include the lentil mixture.

---

¹/₂ cup/125 ml/4 fl oz hot milk
2 tbsp rose water or a few drops rose essence

Dribble the hot milk, the remaining ghee and oil and the rose water over the final layer. Cover with a close-fitting lid to prevent any steam escaping and cook over a low heat for 20 minutes. Remove the pan from the heat and stand on a wet tea-towel. This will help to loosen the crust that will have formed at the bottom of the pot. Allow to stand for 10 minutes. Remove the lid and gently fork through the layers to mix. Or you may wish to retain the layers as far as possible by using a broad spatula to lift carefully and remove to a serving platter.

SAFFRON AND COCONUT-FLAVOURED RICE

Kesari Khichdi

Rice cooked in coconut milk, flavoured and coloured with saffron threads is made more aromatic with the addition of whole spices. Canned coconut milk is available from most supermarkets and oriental food stores, while the orange-red masoor lentils have the advantage of not needing to be soaked before cooking.

1¹/2 cups/350 g/12 oz basmati rice
¹/2 cup/125 g/4 oz masoor lentils
2 cups/500 ml/1 pint water
¹/2 tsp salt

Pick over the rice for grit, then rinse in several changes of water until the water runs clear. Cover the rice with water and soak for 20 minutes. Drain and allow to dry. Set aside.

Pick over the lentils for grit. Rinse in several changes of water until the water runs clear. Put the lentils into a saucepan with the water, add the salt, bring to the boil and simmer for about 5 minutes. Drain and set aside.

---

2 tbsp ghee or vegetable oil
2 finely sliced onions
1 tsp cumin seeds
1 cinnamon stick
1 tsp cardamom seeds
10 cloves

2.5 cm/1 inch grated ginger
3 cloves finely chopped garlic
2 finely chopped green chillies
2 cups/500 ml/1 pint canned coconut milk
1¹/2 cups/375 ml/12 fl oz water
¹/2 tsp saffron threads, steeped for 15 minutes in
2 tbsp warm milk
Salt to taste

Heat the ghee or oil in a heavy-bottomed pan and fry the onions until translucent. Add and stir-fry the cumin, cinnamon, cardamom, cloves, ginger, garlic and chilli until the onion starts to change colour. Then stir in the drained rice and the lentils, the coconut milk, water, saffron threads in milk and salt. Bring to the boil, stir gently once with a wooden spoon and cover with a close-fitting lid. Reduce the heat and simmer. Lift the lid after 10 minutes and fork through, then replace the lid and cook for a further 10 minutes. Fork through gently again, remove from the heat, place a tea-towel over the pan, replace the lid and leave for 10 minutes. Fork onto a serving platter and garnish with a scattering of onion, almonds and raisins.

---

1 tbsp ghee
1 finely sliced onion
1 tbsp slivered almonds
2 tbsp raisins

To make the garnish, heat the ghee and fry the onion until brown, then remove onto absorbent kitchen paper with a slotted spoon. Fry the almonds in the remaining ghee until golden and remove onto absorbent paper. Fry the raisins until they puff up and scatter them, the onions and the almonds over the rice.

TOMATO PILAU

Tamatar Pilau

As children, we were very fond of a rice dish we called Tomato Rice, which was always served with puréed lentils. The flavour of this Tamatar Pilau awakened a childhood memory and it now appears regularly at our table.

2 cups/500 g/1 lb basmati rice
3 tbsp ghee
2 finely sliced onions
1 tsp cumin seeds
1 tsp cardamom seeds
$1/2$ tsp cracked black pepper
5 cm/2 inches cinnamon stick
1 tsp turmeric powder
350 g/12 oz lean lamb, trimmed of fat and cubed
3 large tomatoes, blanched and puréed
1 tbsp malt vinegar

Pick over the rice for grit and stones, then rinse it until the water runs clear. Cover with water and stand for 20 minutes. Drain and allow to dry.

Heat the ghee in a heavy-bottomed pan and fry the onion until it starts to change colour. Add the cumin, cardamom, pepper, cinnamon and turmeric and fry for 3 minutes. Stir in the cubed meat and cook to seal. Then add the puréed tomatoes and vinegar, cover and simmer for about 30 minutes or until the meat is almost cooked. Discard the cinnamon stick.

2 finely diced potatoes
2 tsp salt
3 cups/750 ml/1¹/₂ pints hot water

Add the diced potato, the drained rice, salt and hot water to the meat mixture. Stir well, reduce the heat, cover with a tight-fitting lid and cook for 20 minutes. Remove the lid and fork through gently. Cover the pan with a tea-towel and replace the lid. Leave to stand for 10 minutes. Remove to a serving platter.

1 tbsp ghee
1 finely sliced onion
125 g/4 oz cooked green peas

Fry the onions in hot ghee until they turn brown and crisp. Boil the peas and scatter them and the onion over the surface of the pilau.

BREADS

MANY DIFFERENT BREADS ARE MADE in the home in India, using flours ground from wheat, rice, pulses, corn and root vegetables such as potato and tapioca. The most commonly used is a fine-textured wholemeal flour, which is sold as atta in oriental shops. Atta flour is low in gluten and this makes it easy to knead and roll. It should be finely sieved before use.

The basic dough mixture can take on different guises when other ingredients are incorporated into it. Chopped coriander, chillies, onions or grated coconut may be mixed in individually or together to make for an interestingly flavoured bread. Spiced mashed potato and lentils or spicy minced meat are often used as a filling and placed between a couple of bread circles before being fried.

Most of the popular homemade breads, like chapatis or rotlis, are unleavened flat breads either made into a disc with a rolling pin or flattened and formed by hand. They are eaten at almost every meal, and often served alongside rice. A cast iron griddle called a *tawa* is heated on an open flame and the breads are dry-cooked on the hot griddle, while the pooris are deep-fried and inflate like a balloon. Leavened bread such as naan, popular in Moghul and north Indian cooking, is generally considered by Parsis to be too filling and difficult to digest in the hot climate of Gujarat.

WHEAT FLOUR FLAT BREAD

Ghan Ni Rotli

Most of the breads or rotlis enjoyed by Parsis are those commonly encountered in India, such as chapatis, pooris, parathas or kulchas. There are, however, two types of bread attributed specifically to Parsi cuisine, this one, made from wheat flour, and that which follows, which is made with rice flour. A lighter dough results when boiling water is used, and the rotli is lighter still if hot milk is used. These breads will remain soft for several hours and may be eaten warm or cold.

---

280 g/10 oz/2¼ cups wheat flour
½ tsp salt
4–6 tbsp boiling water
1½ tbsp melted ghee
Flour for dusting

Sift the flour into a bowl and mix in the salt. Make a well in the centre and add the melted ghee. Using a wooden spoon to mix, add sufficient boiling water and stir well into the mixture. When the mixture has cooled sufficiently to allow you to work it, knead to a pliable dough, sprinkling over a little more water if necessary.

1 tbsp melted ghee

Divide the dough into 12 portions and roll into balls. Flatten the balls. Dust a rolling surface with flour and roll out the dough balls one at a time into thin rounds. Heat a flat griddle and place a rotli on it, pressing the upper surface gently with a spatula to form air bubbles. Turn over and repeat until most of the surface has bubbled. Remove and brush with melted ghee. Fold in half or roll to form a cylinder.

RICE FLOUR FLAT BREAD

Doodh Rotli

This flat bread can be made with boiling water, but the combination of boiled milk and rice flour results in a softer, lighter bread. You will need to keep turning the dough discs on the hot griddle because the fine rice flour burns more easily than wheat flour. The amount of liquid required depends on the texture of the flour.

280 g/10 oz/2¼ cups fine rice flour
½ tsp salt
4–6 tbsp boiling milk

Rice flour for dusting

Sift the flour and salt into a bowl. Gradually add boiling milk as required and mix with a wooden spoon to bind. When the mixture has cooled, knead it well to a pliable dough and form into 12 balls. Flatten the balls, dust a rolling surface with rice flour and roll the balls out one at a time into thin rounds. Heat a flat griddle and place a rotli on it, pressing the upper surface gently with a spatula to form air bubbles. Turn over frequently and repeat until most of the surface has bubbled. Do not allow to burn.

BALLOONED BREAD CIRCLES

Pooris

Unlike chapatis and other rotlis, which are cooked on a hot griddle, pooris are deep-fried. Air enters the pooris during the cooking process and they balloon up, rising to the surface of the hot ghee or oil. Hot pooris are traditionally used to scoop up Pistachio and Almond Pudding (p.166), and they are also eaten with spiced savoury meat or vegetable dishes. Three types of flour are used in this recipe.

350 g/12 oz/1¹/2 cups plain flour
250 g/8 oz/1 cup wholemeal flour
2 tbsp semolina
1 tsp salt
1 tbsp ghee
200–250 ml/6–8 fl oz/³/4–1 cup hot water
Plain flour for dusting

Sift the plain and wholemeal flours into a bowl, stir in the semolina and salt, and rub in the ghee. Add hot water as required and knead into a stiff dough. Continue to knead for about 10 minutes or until the dough becomes pliable. Cover and set aside for 1 hour. Knead the dough once again. Form the dough into 12 balls. Dust a rolling surface with flour and roll the balls out one at a time into thin rounds. Cover with a damp cloth to keep moist while continuing with the frying procedure.

Ghee or vegetable oil for deep-frying

Heat the ghee or oil in a heavy-bottomed pan until it begins to smoke. Then reduce the heat to a minimum and slip in the pooris one at a time, pressing them down gently with a spatula. Lift the spatula almost immediately and the poori will rise to the top, flip it over and stroke or press the disc to encourage ballooning. Fry for a few seconds and flip over once again. When light gold in colour remove with a slotted spoon to drain on absorbent paper. Serve immediately or keep the pooris in a warm oven and serve hot. They will deflate, but this does not detract from the flavour.

SWEET POORIS

Mitthi Pooris

Simple to prepare, these pooris are popular as a tea-time snack or as welcome-home fare for hungry schoolchildren. Once the dough is prepared, cover it with a damp cloth and set to rest in a warm place. In India fresh grated coconut would be used to flavour these pooris. If you use desiccated coconut, soften it with a little water before adding it to the dough. If you prefer, the pooris may also be flavoured with almond or vanilla essence. Vegetable oil may be used for the deep-frying, but ghee gives a nice buttery flavour to the pooris.

---

120 g/4 oz/¹/₂ cup self-raising flour
120 g/4 oz/¹/₂ cup semolina
1 tsp melted ghee
60 g/2 oz sugar
A pinch of salt
125 ml/4 fl oz rose water or a few drops of rose essence
2 tbsp freshly grated or desiccated coconut
Flour for dusting

Sieve the flour into a bowl, add the semolina and rub in the melted ghee. Add the sugar, salt and rose water and knead well into a firm dough. You may need to sprinkle a little water into the dough when kneading. Cover with a damp cloth and set to rest in a warm place for about 1 hour. Pinch the dough off into about 16 pieces and roll into balls. Dust a rolling surface with flour and roll the balls out into thin circles.

Ghee or vegetable oil for deep-frying

Heat the ghee or oil until a haze rises and deep-fry the pooris one or two at a time. They will rise to the surface and puff up. Use a spatula to turn them once and continue to fry until they become very light gold in colour. Remove to absorbent paper to drain. The pooris are best served immediately, while puffed up. Some may deflate, but they will still be tasty.

DESSERTS AND PASTRIES

MOST PARSIS, LIKE THE GREAT MAJORITY of Indians, are sweet-toothed, and no meal would be considered complete unless followed by a dessert or sweetmeat, while confections and pastries are also often served at tea-time. Many households have a supply of sweet offerings permanently to hand with which to welcome visitors at any time of the day, whether expected or otherwise.

Sweet-making falls into many categories and can include sweets immersed in syrup, biscuit-like pastries, rich halvas, fudges, toffee and puddings. Many dessert preparations are milk-based, often in the form of milk thickened and reduced by boiling to which other ingredients such as semolina or vermicelli may be added. Fruit, nuts and raisins, together with spices such as cardamom and nutmeg, provide flavouring and texture, while saffron and rose essence or rose water are added for both fragrance and flavour. To some people in the West, the very word semolina conjures up memories of stodgy school food, but not in India, where semolina is widely used to make delicacies such as Rose-Flavoured Festive Pudding (p.161) and Almond and Raisin Dessert (p.155).

Many Indian sweet dishes are time-consuming to prepare, and throughout the country there are specialist sweet-makers known as *halvais* from whom households will often purchase sweetmeats, puddings and desserts rather than cooking them at home. This chapter includes a wide variety of recipes and I do hope that you will attempt some, such as the Almond Honey Brittle (p.146), to be stored and offered to unexpected guests and others, like the rich Wedding Custard (p.150), to be prepared for special and auspicious occasions.

ALMOND HONEY BRITTLE

Gaz

This brittle is sweetened with both sugar and honey and flavoured with saffron and rose essence or water. It is to be found in many variations all along the Silk Route to the Middle East.

You will need to grease a flat tray or oven platter ready to take the brittle. The drops of the mixture need to be spaced to allow for some spreading, so, depending on their size, you may need one or two trays.

200 g/7 oz sugar
4 tbsp honey
2 tbsp ghee
2 tbsp vegetable oil
125 g/4 oz blanched and slivered almonds
60 g/2 oz blanched and roughly chopped pistachios
1/2 tsp saffron threads, steeped for 15 minutes in
1 tbsp hot water
1/2 tsp rose essence or 1 tbsp rose water

Bring the sugar, honey, ghee and oil to the boil in a heavy-bottomed saucepan and stir until the sugar has dissolved. Add the almonds and pistachios and stir for about 2 minutes or until the mixture becomes firm and turns light gold in colour. Then stir in the saffron threads and the rose essence or water and cook for a further 3 minutes, stirring occasionally. The mixture will become a golden brown. Do not allow it to darken too much or it will acquire a bitter taste. Have a bowl of iced water ready next to the stove and drop a little of the mixture into the water as it turns golden brown. When the drops harden immediately in the cold water, the brittle is ready.

Ghee or butter for greasing

Lightly grease a flat tray and place teaspoonfuls of the mixture onto the tray leaving about 2.5cm/1 inch between each piece. Allow to cool and store in an airtight container.

BANANA FRITTERS

Kervai

There are two methods of preparing these walnut-shaped banana fritters, which are usually served at tea-time. The ingredients are the same in both, but in one method the nuts and raisins, instead of being sealed into the centre of the banana balls, are incorporated with all the other ingredients into the banana pulp.

6 large well ripened bananas
3 tbsp cornflour

Peel the bananas and cut them in half lengthwise. Lightly scrape out the central core and mash the bananas to a smooth pulp with the cornflour. Set aside.

2 tbsp ghee
60 g/2 oz blanched and slivered almonds
60 g/2 oz seeded raisins

Heat the ghee and fry the almonds until they are light gold in colour. Remove the nuts with a slotted spoon the moment they change colour, as they burn very easily. If burning does occur, discard the almonds and start again. Toss and fry the raisins in the remaining ghee until they puff up, remove them with a slotted spoon and set aside.

1 tbsp poppy seeds
1 tsp cardamom powder

¹/2 tsp nutmeg powder
3 tbsp sugar
Vegetable oil for deep-frying

Mix together the poppy seeds, cardamom, nutmeg and sugar and sprinkle over the fried almonds and raisins.

Form the banana pulp into walnut-sized balls, make a small depression in each ball and fill with the nut and raisin mixture; close the depression carefully and reform the ball. Then deep-fry in hot oil, turning the balls gently until they become golden brown in colour.

CARROT HALVA

Gajarpak

Different versions of this halva appear in many of India's regional cuisines. Halvas are made from a variety of ingredients ranging from beetroot to dates, while others are flour-based, using semolina and flavoured with spices such as cardamom and nutmeg. In India the type of carrot used for this recipe would be much deeper in colour than those available in the West, and the halva would be almost red rather than orange.

750 g/1¹/2 lb carrots
4 cups/1 litre/2 pints milk
³/4 cup/150 ml/5 fl oz cream
150 g/5 oz sugar
3 tbsp ghee

Peel and dice the carrots and boil them in *un*salted water until soft. Discard the water in which they have been cooked and mash to a purée consistency. Return to the heat, add the milk, cream and sugar and stir and simmer until the mixture thickens. Finally, stir in the ghee. Set aside to cool.

3 eggs
1¹/2 tsp cardamom powder
1¹/2 tsp nutmeg powder

Beat the eggs together and stir into the carrot mixture. Then stir in the cardamom and nutmeg powder. Return the pan to a low heat and stir gently but continuously until the mixture pulls away from the sides of the pan. Remove to a serving platter. Serve warm or cold with a swirl of cream.

WEDDING CUSTARD

Lagan Nu Custard

Baked custards are a great favourite with Parsis and no wedding banquet would be considered complete without one. In this version the mashed pumpkin gives an additional dimension to both the taste and texture of the dish. If you can't buy charoli nuts, almonds may be substituted.

250 g/8 oz chopped pumpkin

Cover the pumpkin with *un*salted water and boil for approximately 10 minutes or until it can be mashed easily against the side of the pan. Drain and set aside.

---

2 cups/¹/2 litre/16 fl oz milk
3 tbsp sugar
¹/2 tsp rose essence or 1 tbsp rose water

Add the sugar to the milk and bring to the boil, reduce the heat and simmer for 10 minutes. Mix in the mashed pumpkin and the rose essence or water and simmer for a further 5 minutes. Set aside to cool.

3–4 eggs
2 tbsp milk
2 tbsp finely crushed almonds
1 tsp cardamom powder
¹/2 tsp nutmeg powder
1 tbsp butter
2 tbsp charoli nuts or finely crushed almonds

Beat the eggs and milk together and mix into the pumpkin mixture. Add the crushed almonds, cardamom and nutmeg and stir well to mix. Pour into a greased baking dish allowing a little space for the mixture to rise. Sprinkle the crushed charoli nuts over the surface and bake in an oven pre-heated to 200°C/425°F/gas mark 6 for 20 minutes or until the surface begins to brown.

WHITE GOURD HALVA

Dodhi No Halwa

The appearance of this dish is enlivened by adding a colouring agent, while the flavouring can be varied by using vanilla essence instead of the rose essence or rose water. This halva may be served hot as a dessert or cut into squares when cold and served as a sweetmeat.

---

1 kg/2 lb peeled and grated white gourd
4 cups/1 litre/1³/4 pints milk
250 g/8 oz sugar
30 g/1 oz finely chopped blanched almonds
30 g/1 oz finely chopped blanched pistachios
60 g/2 oz butter
1 tbsp rose water or ¹/2 tsp rose essence
1 tsp cardamom powder
3–4 drops green food colouring (optional)

Place the grated gourd in a heavy-bottomed pan, add the milk and sugar and bring to the boil. Then lower the heat and simmer for about 45 minutes, stirring occasionally to prevent sticking. Add the chopped almonds, pistachios, butter, rose water or essence and cardamom, and continue to simmer and stir until the mixture thickens and begins to pull away from the sides of the pan. Add the colouring.

Ghee or butter to grease the platter

Spread the mixture on a greased platter and allow to cool. Refrigerate and cut into squares when cold.

CARDAMOM-FLAVOURED PASTRIES

Meethi Papdi

These sweet cardomom-flavoured discs, which I usually serve dusted with icing sugar, may be eaten at tea-time or with after-dinner coffee. When I was first given them in a Parsi home, they accompanied Almond and Semolina Dessert (p.155), which was spooned onto the papdis.

---

200 g/7 oz plain flour, plus extra to dust
2¹/₂ tbsp melted ghee
125 g/4 oz sugar
1 tsp cardamom powder
4 beaten egg yolks
Milk sufficient to make a smooth dough

Sift the flour into a bowl and mix in the ghee, sugar, cardamom and egg yolks. Gradually add the milk and knead to a soft dough. Cover the bowl and set aside for 1 hour. Knead again lightly. Dust a rolling surface and rolling pin with flour, roll out the dough and cut it into circles about 6.5 cm/2¹/₂ inches in diameter. Prick through with a fork to prevent the circles puffing up when fried.

Ghee for deep-frying

Heat the ghee and fry the papdis a few at a time, turning them occasionally. Remove onto absorbent paper as they start to change colour.

DATE AND ALMOND PASTRY PARCELS

Khajoor Ni Ghari

This tasty confection can be enjoyed at tea-time or served with coffee after dinner. Dates are rich in vitamins and proteins and have a high sugar content, which explains the absence of cane sugar in this recipe.

350 g/12 oz pitted dates
1 tsp cardamom powder
1 tsp nutmeg powder
30 g/1 oz flaked almonds

Blend the dates with the cardamom and nutmeg in a food-processor. Mix the flaked almonds into the date paste and set aside.

150 g/5 oz wholemeal or atta flour
1 tbsp plain flour
1¹/₂ tbsp rice flour
1¹/₂ tbsp ghee
¹/₄ tsp salt
30 g/1 oz slivered almonds

Sift the wholemeal, plain and rice flours into a bowl and mix together. Rub the ghee and the salt into the flours and mix to a soft dough with a little water. Knead well.

Divide the dough into small balls the size of walnuts. Make a depression and fill with the date mixture, pressing a couple of slivered almonds onto the paste. Pinch the dough together to close the hollow to flatten or roll the balls out into circles 5 mm/ ¹/4 inch thick.

Ghee for shallow-frying

Heat the ghee in a frying pan, reduce the heat and shallow-fry each ghari until it is golden on both sides. They can be eaten either warm or cold.

ALMOND AND RAISIN DESSERT

Malido

There are several versions of this rich dessert, and this one is traditionally served either hot or cold with Cardamom-Flavoured Pastries (p.153). Charoli nuts are tiny rounded seed kernels slightly smaller than pistachios used to top many Indian desserts and are sometimes available from oriental shops. They have a flavour similar to almonds, which may be used as a substitute.

2 tbsp ghee
50 g/2 oz blanched and slivered almonds
30 g/1 oz seedless raisins

Heat the ghee in a small pan and toss the almonds in it until they turn gold in colour. Remove with a slotted spoon. Add the raisins to the remaining ghee and toss them until they begin to puff up. Remove and set aside with the almonds.

4 tbsp ghee
2 cups/500 g/1 lb medium-milled semolina

Add 4 tablespoons of ghee to whatever ghee remains in the pan and fry the semolina, stirring constantly until it is gold in colour. Set aside.

---

125 g/4 oz sugar
1/2 cup/125 ml/4 fl oz water
4 beaten eggs
1 tsp rose essence or 2 tbsp rose water
1 tsp cardamom powder
1 tsp nutmeg powder
10 g/1/2 oz charoli nuts (optional)

Bring the sugar and water to the boil in a heavy-bottomed pan and stir while boiling until the sugar melts. Set aside to cool.

When the syrup has cooled, gradually stir in the beaten eggs and the semolina and beat vigorously. Return the pan to the heat and continue to stir until the ghee begins to separate out from the mixture. Remove from the heat and stir in the rose essence, cardamom, nutmeg and the charoli nuts.

ALMOND FUDGE

Eeda Pakh

This is a rich fudge, laden with eggs and butter, and it keeps well in the refrigerator for several weeks. The flavours are enhanced when the fudge is slightly warmed before serving.

6 lightly beaten eggs
250 g/8 oz sugar
5 generous tbsp ground almonds
2 generous tbsp ground pine kernels
125 g/4 oz melted butter
1 tsp rose essence or 2 tbsp rose water
1 tsp cardamom powder
1/2 tsp nutmeg powder
3 tbsp thick cream

Put the beaten eggs, almonds, pine kernels, butter, rose essence, cardamom, nutmeg and cream into a heavy-bottomed, non-stick pan and stir well to mix all the ingredients together. Then put on a low heat while stirring constantly to avoid the egg forming lumps on the bottom. The mixture needs to become thick and pull away from the sides of the pan. This could take some time depending on the size and thickness of the pan.

Butter for greasing
2 tbsp finely chopped almonds mixed with
1 tbsp finely chopped pine kernels

Grease a baking tin approximately 18–20 cm/7–8 inches square and transfer the mixture into it. Flatten the surface of the fudge mixture, and scatter and lightly press the mixed nuts over the top. Allow to cool slightly and mark into squares or diamond shapes. When completely cool, cut right through and remove from the baking tin.

CREAMY VERMICELLI WITH NUTS AND RAISINS

Sev

In India, vermicelli are used in both sweet and savoury dishes. Here, fine vermicelli strands are first fried in ghee and then sweetened and simmered gently until all the strands are separated. Finally, flavourings are added along with almonds and raisins.

Strange though it may seem to some western readers, this pudding, which may be served warm or chilled, is often eaten with hard-boiled eggs in India.

3 tbsp ghee or butter
30 g/1oz blanched and slivered almonds
30 g/1oz seedless raisins or sultanas

Heat the butter or ghee in a heavy-bottomed pan, add the almonds and fry to a light golden colour. Remove with a slotted spoon onto absorbent kitchen paper. Then add the raisins to the remaining ghee and fry until they puff up; remove to drain with the almonds.

125 g/4 oz fine vermicelli, broken into 5 cm/2 inch lengths
4–6 tbsp sugar dissolved in a little water
1 cup/250 ml/8 fl oz milk
2 tbsp pouring cream
1/2 tsp nutmeg powder
1 tsp cardamom powder
1/2 tsp rose essence or 1 tbsp rose water

Add the vermicelli to the remaining ghee and stir and fry until the noodles change colour. Drain off any excess ghee and return the pan to a low heat, add the dissolved sugar, milk and cream to cover the vermicelli and simmer until the liquid is almost absorbed and the strands are separate. Then mix in the almonds, raisins, nutmeg, cardamom and rose essence or water and continue to simmer for about 1 minute.

RICH CUSTARD

Lagan Nu Kastar

That the Parsis are fond of egg dishes is nowhere better demonstrated than in their custard preparations. This delicious dessert is rich with cream and eggs and has delicate vanilla and rose flavours. Rose water is a dilution of the essence or oils of roses and can be used more liberally than rose essence, which is very strong. Rose water is more easily obtainable from both chemists and oriental shops.

2 cups / ¹/₂ litre / 18 fl oz milk
125 g / 4 oz sugar

Bring the milk to the boil in a heavy-bottomed pan, add the sugar and stir until the sugar is dissolved. Lower the heat and simmer until the milk reduces to half its quantity. Allow to cool.

———————

4 lightly beaten eggs
¹/₂ cup / 125 ml / 4 fl oz pouring cream
30 g / 1 oz blanched and slivered almonds
¹/₂ tsp caraway seeds
1 tsp nutmeg powder
1 tsp vanilla essence
1 tsp rose essence or 2 tbsp rosewater

Add the beaten eggs, cream, almonds, caraway seeds, nutmeg, vanilla essence and rosewater or rose essence to the milk.

———————

30 g / 1 oz butter
1 tbsp chopped charoli nuts or almonds

Liberally grease an oven-proof dish, deep enough to allow the mixture to rise slightly, with the butter. Pour the mixture into the dish, sprinkle with nuts and bake it in an oven pre-heated to 180°C/350°F/gas mark 4 for 35 minutes. The surface should set to a light golden colour.

ROSE-FLAVOURED FESTIVE PUDDING

Ravo

This dessert flavoured with rose, cardamom and nutmeg is often served on festive and auspicious occasions. Milk is sweetened and boiled until it is reduced in quantity and then further thickened with semolina. It is tasty and easy to prepare and may be eaten either warm or cold.

---

3 tbsp ghee or butter
30 g/1 oz blanched and chopped almonds
30 g/1 oz sultanas
5 tbsp semolina

Heat the ghee or butter in a heavy-bottomed pan, stir-fry the nuts and sultanas until the nuts are a light gold colour. Remove the almonds and sultanas with a slotted spoon and set aside. Add the semolina to the remaining ghee or butter and stir constantly until it begins to change colour. Do not allow it to darken and burn. Set aside.

---

5 tbsp sugar
4 cups/1 litre/1³/4 pints milk
1 egg
2 tbsp milk
1 tsp cardamom powder
1 tsp nutmeg powder
1 tbsp rose water or ¹/2 tsp rose essence

Add the sugar to the milk in a heavy-bottomed saucepan, bring to the boil, lower the heat and simmer, stirring occasionally until the milk is reduced to half its original quantity. Then mix in the fried semolina and stir briskly to prevent lumps forming. Add a little more milk if the mixture becomes too thick.

Whisk the egg into the milk and add gradually to the semolina mixture while stirring briskly. Lower the heat and stir in the almonds and sultanas, the cardamom, nutmeg and rose water or rose essence.

SAFFRON-FLAVOURED PASTRIES

Dahitran

Children love these pastries flavoured with rose and saffron. Yoghurt is used as the raising agent and you will need to allow at least 2 hours for the dough to rise. The syrup has to be quite thick in order to coat the deep-fried pastries. When cooled, the syrup should have a sticky, toffee-like consistency.

140 g/4 1/2 oz plain flour
140 g/4 1/2 oz semolina
2 tbsp ghee
2 tbsp yoghurt
1 tsp cardamom powder
Salt to taste
1/2 tsp saffron threads steeped in
2 tbsp warm milk for 15 minutes

Sift the flour and the semolina into a bowl. Then add the ghee, yoghurt, cardamom, salt and the saffron threads in milk and knead well. Leave the dough to rise in a warm place for 2–3 hours. Meanwhile, you may wish to prepare the syrup. Then knead the dough again – it may be necessary to sprinkle the dough with a little milk to keep it moist.

Dust a work surface with flour and roll the dough out to a thickness of 1.25 cm/½ inch and use a mould or wine glass to cut it into rounds.

Ghee for deep-frying
500 g/1 lb sugar
1½ cups/375 ml/12 fl oz water
1½ tsp rose essence or 3 tbsp rose water

Heat the ghee and deep-fry the dahitrans until golden brown. Remove to drain and cool on kitchen paper.

Make a thick syrup with the sugar and water and add the rose essence or water to the syrup. Drop the dahitrans into the warm syrup and remove when they start settling at the bottom of the syrup.

NUT BITES

Bhakhra

Serve these bites as a tea-time snack or with after-dinner coffee. Lightly spiced with cardamom and nutmeg, the nutty flavours of almonds and pistachios are given another taste dimension with the addition of caraway seeds. I sometimes ring the changes by substituting fennel for caraway, which makes a flavoursome alternative.

Drain the yoghurt of whey through a cheesecloth or muslin over a bowl. This will take a couple of hours or may be left overnight in the refrigerator.

------

350 g/12 oz plain flour
125 g/4 oz semolina
1¹/₂ tsp baking powder
1 tbsp ghee
3 lightly beaten eggs
400 g/14 oz sugar
125 g/4 oz blanched and ground almonds
75 g/3 oz blanched and ground pistachios
1 tbsp caraway seeds
2 tsp cardamom powder
1 tsp nutmeg powder
¹/₂ cup yoghurt, drained of whey

Mix the sifted flour with the semolina and baking powder. Then rub in the ghee and add the beaten eggs, sugar, ground almonds and pistachios, caraway seeds, cardamom and nutmeg powder and the drained yoghurt. Knead to a dough, place in a cloth-covered bowl and set aside to rise for between 1 and 1¹/₂ hours. When the dough has risen, knead it lightly and roll out on a floured surface to a thickness of 5 mm/¹/₄ inch and cut into shapes with a biscuit cutter.

Ghee for deep-frying

Heat the ghee in a heavy-bottomed pan and deep-fry the doughshapes a few at a time for about 2 minutes on each side until golden brown. Remove with a slotted spoon and drain on absorbent paper.

PUFFS OF MILK

Doodh Na Puffs

When I was first told about 'puffs of milk' I thought I was having my leg pulled, but the puffs are really froths of milk. 'When stirring the milk,' I was told, 'you should do so either clockwise or anticlockwise, but never in both directions. The milk has to be boiled and then left to cool overnight in the refrigerator. Preparation must take place before sunrise because the heat of the day will cause the puffs to sag. Serve it immediately as a pre-breakfast drink.' And a word of caution was added: 'When beating the milk, never let the beater touch the bottom of the vessel, nor should it be held in the dead centre – otherwise the puffs (or froth) will never rise and will start sagging.'

Serve in tall glasses. Vanilla or almond essence may be substituted for the rose essence.

---

3 cups / 700 ml / 1¼ pints milk
175 g / 6 oz sugar

Add the sugar to the milk, bring it to the boil in a deep pan and then keep on a rolling boil for 10 minutes. Remove from the heat and stir from time to time while cooling. When cool, cover with muslin or cheesecloth dampened with iced water and refrigerate overnight.

---

2 tbsp rose water or 1 tsp rose essence
Nutmeg powder

Early the next morning, add the rose water or essence to the milk and beat with a rotary beater until the froth forms. Carefully remove the froth only as it forms with a large spoon and fill each glass to form a peak at the brim. Continue beating and removing the froth to fill the glass. Finally, sprinkle each frothy peak with a generous pinch of nutmeg powder.

PISTACHIO AND ALMOND PUDDING

Doodh Pak

'*Doodh*' means milk and '*pak*' means sweet. This sweet milk dish is traditionally served with Ballooned Bread Circles (p.142). Egg whites only are beaten to a froth – the yolks may be used for a dish like Minced Lamb with Liver (p.62).

4 cups/1 litre/1³/4 pints milk
200 g/6 oz sugar
2 egg whites

Place the milk in a heavy-bottomed pan, add the sugar and bring to the boil. Then lower the heat and stir and simmer until the quantity is reduced by about one third. Remove from the heat.

Separate the egg yolks from the whites, whisk the whites to a froth and add to the sweetened and reduced milk, stirring constantly. Return the pan to a low heat and continue stirring until the mixture thickens.

125 g/4 oz finely ground blanched almonds
60 g/2 oz finely ground blanched pistachios
2 tsp cardamom powder
1/2 tsp nutmeg powder
1 tsp rose essence or 1 tbsp rose water

While stirring, add the ground almonds, pistachios, cardamom, nutmeg and rose essence or water, stir to blend and heat through. Remove from the heat, allow to cool and serve with hot Pooris (p.143).

CASHEWNUT TOFFEE

Kaju Nikatri

You will need to grease a flat platter in order to make this simple cashewnut toffee. Work swiftly to mix the nuts, cardamom and essence into the toffee and pour and spread immediately onto the platter.

500 g/1 lb sugar
250 ml/8 fl oz/1 cup water
1 tsp malt vinegar

Add the sugar and vinegar to the water in a heavy-bottomed pan, bring to the boil, lower the heat and stir and simmer until the sugar is dissolved and the syrup thickens. To test, drop a little into cold water – it should form a hard ball.

500 g/1 lb finely chopped cashewnuts
1 tsp cardamom powder
1/2 tsp rose or vanilla essence
Ghee or butter for greasing

Stir the chopped cashews, cardamom powder and the vanilla essence into the syrup and pour the mixture immediately onto the greased platter. Cut into squares or diamonds whilst still hot. Allow to cool and store in an airtight container.

FIRM-TEXTURED ICE CREAM

Kulfi

Indian ice cream is quite different to its Western cousin, which is often thickened with egg yolks or gelatine. In kulfi, the milk is boiled down until it reduces to a thick, creamy texture. Apart from chopped nuts such as pistachios and almonds, kulfi can also be flavoured with puréed mango or saffron. Nowadays, kulfi is normally bought ready-made, but there is always something special about the homemade version, which more than deserves its place in a collection of Parsi recipes.

10 cups/2 1/4 litres/5 pints milk
125 g/4 oz sugar
1 cup double cream
125 g/4 oz blanched and finely chopped pistachios
2 tbsp rose water or
a few drops of rose or vanilla essence

Mix the sugar, milk and cream together in a heavy-bottomed pan and boil until the milk thickens or condenses to half the original quantity. This can take some considerable time. Keep stirring across the bottom of the pan to avoid sticking and scorching. Remove from the heat and allow to cool. When cold, add the pistachios and rose water. Freeze in individual moulds or ice-block trays. Remove from the freezer shortly before serving to allow the kulfi to soften slightly, making it easier to release from the mould.

CHUTNEYS, SALADS AND SAUCES

CHUTNEYS AND PICKLES are always served as accompaniments to an Indian meal, whether Kashmiri or Keralan, Hindu or Parsi. They serve to sharpen the taste buds, and are made from a wide variety of ingredients including fruit, vegetables and herbs, even prawns and fish. They can be sweetened with sugar, made spicy with chilli, sweet and sour with tamarind or tart with vinegar made from dates, sugar cane or toddy. Because pickles and chutneys are everyday fare, they are made in large quantities from fresh fruits and vegetables to be stored and consumed until the next season. Today, supermarket shelves display every imaginable type of pickle and chutney, but in India there is still a great sense of pride attached to making these items in the home.

Chutney is an anglicised version of the Hindi word '*chatni*', and some chutneys, such as the those using coconut as their principal ingredient (p.171 and p.176), are freshly ground to be served immediately, while others, like the Green Mango and Pineapple Chutney (p.173), require fruits to be cooked to a jam-like consistency. Pickles tend to be more spicy and in most recipes vinegar is an important ingredient, providing the necessary tartness and also acting as a preservative.

Raitas are popular cooling agents, made from yoghurt to which finely chopped or grated vegetables such as raw carrot, cucumber or onion are added. Cooked vegetables, for example beetroot or potatoes cut into small cubes, may be used, and there are also raitas made with fruit such as chopped banana or grapes. This chapter includes a yoghurt-based sauce (p.172) that goes well with rice dishes and kedgerees as well as a salad-type dish (p.175), which is a more or less compulsory accompaniment to dhansaks.

COCONUT CHUTNEY

Nariyal Ni Chutney

This condiment is easy to prepare, tasty and pleasing to the eye. Mint and coriander leaves are blended together with coconut and the result is a lovely pale shade of green. The paste looks very cooling, but beware – a powerful chilli flavour lies beneath its calm surface. Coconut grated fresh and then frozen can now be found in some oriental shops.

75 g/2¹/₂ oz desiccated or grated fresh coconut
2 green chillies

6 cloves chopped garlic
1¹/₂ cups chopped coriander leaves
¹/₂ cup chopped mint leaves
4 tsp sugar
1¹/₂ tsp salt
3 tbsp lime or lemon juice

Blend all the ingredients to a thick paste.

SPICY YOGHURT SAUCE

Dahi Ni Kadhi

This thin yoghurt sauce laced with garlic, chilli and spices is a favourite with vegetarians, and helps to liven up either khichdi or plain white rice. It also makes an ideal accompaniment for more complex dishes like Orange-Flavoured Rice with Dates (p.132).

2 tbsp ghee
2 tsp cumin seeds
1 tsp mustard seeds
4 cloves
1 finely chopped onion
6 cloves finely chopped garlic
2 tsp finely chopped ginger
3 finely chopped green chillies
10 curry leaves
¹/₂ tsp turmeric powder

1 tsp sugar
1 tbsp chick-pea flour, mixed into a paste with a little water
Salt to taste

Heat the ghee in a heavy-bottomed pan. Add the cumin, mustard seeds and cloves and fry for a few seconds until they begin to splutter and pop and release their aromas. Then add the onion, garlic, ginger, chilli and curry leaves and stir-fry until the onion starts to change colour. Mix in the turmeric powder, sugar, salt and chick-pea flour paste and cook for 1 minute. Remove the pan from the heat.

---

5 cups/1¼ litres/2 pints yoghurt
½ cup finely chopped coriander leaves

Beat the yoghurt well and gradually mix into the cooked ingredients, along with the coriander leaves. Return the pan to the heat and bring to the boil. Reduce the heat and allow to simmer gently for about 3 minutes.

GREEN MANGO AND PINEAPPLE CHUTNEY

Aambakalio

This jam-like dish combines green or unripened mangoes with pineapple and is sweetened with palm sugar. It is served with dhansak dishes and also eaten with bread at breakfast time. *Jaggery* or *gur* (palm sugar) is unprocessed sugar and is compressed into a crudely shaped brown mass; it can sometimes be found in oriental shops. Use brown sugar if palm sugar is unobtainable.

---

175 g/6 oz palm sugar

Grate the palm sugar, cover with hot water and steep to dissolve the sugar. This may also be done over a low heat. Strain through a fine sieve or cheesecloth to remove any grit or impurities and set aside. If you can't find palm sugar, dissolve 1½ cups/375 g/ 12 oz of brown sugar in ½ cup of hot water.

---

2 tbsp ghee
6 finely chopped shallots or small onions
3 medium-sized green mangoes, peeled and diced
2 cups fresh diced pineapple (approximately
²/₃ of a small pineapple)

Heat the ghee in a heavy-bottomed pan and fry the shallots or onions until they start to change colour.

Add the diced fruit and the sugar syrup and simmer until the syrup thickens and the mixture has the consistency of jam. Allow to cool and store in sterilised jars.

TANGY SALAD

Kachubar

This salad is often served with Parsi meals and is an almost obligatory accompaniment to dhansak dishes. Tamarind juice sometimes replaces the lime or lemon juice, and imparts a slightly different tanginess to the dish.

Fresh turmeric is not always easily available and may be omitted. Turmeric powder is *not* a substitute.

3 *finely sliced onions*
2 *tbsp roughly chopped coriander leaves*
2 *finely chopped green chillies*
5 *cm/2 inches finely chopped ginger*
1 *diced cucumber*
2 *diced tomatoes*
$^1/_2$ tsp sea salt
2.5 *cm/1 inch fresh turmeric, grated*
2 *tbsp lime or lemon juice*

Put all the ingredients, except the lime or lemon juice, into a glass serving bowl or dish, fork together gently to mix and then dribble over the lime or lemon juice.

TAMARIND-FLAVOURED COCONUT CHUTNEY

Nariyal Ni Chutney

This chutney is usually served with snacks and freshly made as required, rather than being kept in storage jars, although I have kept it in the fridge without any problems.

1 tbsp tamarind pulp soaked in $^1/_2$ cup water

Steep the tamarind pulp in the hot water. When the water has cooled, squeeze and rub the pulp between your fingers and thumb to dissolve the tamarind. Strain through a sieve and retain the liquid. Discard the solids and set aside.

4 tbsp desiccated or fresh grated coconut
2.5 cm/1 inch roughly chopped ginger
4 cloves garlic
3 roughly chopped green chillies
1 roughly chopped small onion
1 cup chopped coriander leaves
Salt to taste

Blend the coconut, ginger, garlic, chilli, onion, coriander leaves, salt and the reserved tamarind juice to a paste in a food-processor.

LIME AND DATE CHUTNEY

Limbu Ni Chutney

Limes are salted and dried in the sun before being bottled, often in vinegar, in traditional Persian cookery, and it seems likely that both this and the following recipe have their origins in the land the Parsis left more than 1,000 years ago.

If you can, use unwaxed limes to make this distinctive sweet and sour chutney.

16 limes
125 g/4 oz salt

Wash the limes, cut them into quarters and remove the pips. Mix the salt into the limes and place them in a wide-necked glass jar with a non-corrosive lid. Allow to stand for 3 days, shaking the limes around each day. On the fourth day, place the limes on a non-metallic platter, cover with muslin or cheesecloth and leave in a sunny position for 2 days.

1 kg/2 lb soft brown sugar
500 g/1 lb pitted dates
1 tbsp chilli powder
1/2 cup malt vinegar

Blend the limes with the sugar, dates, chilli powder and vinegar in a food-processor and store in glass or earthenware jars.

SALTED LIMES WITH DATES

Limboo Ni Chutney

You will need to allow six days for the limes to soften in the salted juices. Shake the jar quite vigorously several times each day to make sure the limes are being well moistened with the juices. I have occasionally substituted small lemons when limes are out of season and the result has been very satisfactory. If you can, use unwaxed limes.

25 limes
125 g / 4 oz salt
2 tbsp pitted dates
4 cm / 1¹/2 inches grated ginger
3 cloves finely chopped garlic

Wash the limes, cut them into quarters and remove the pips. Rub the salt into the lime pieces and place them in a wide-necked jar with a non-corrosive lid. Leave for six days, but shake the container a couple of times each day to rotate the limes in the salted juice which will increase in quantity as the juice is drawn out of the limes.

After six days, drain off the liquid. Blend the limes, dates, ginger and garlic together in a food-processor and set aside.

750 ml / 1¹/4 pints malt vinegar
500 g / 1lb palm or soft brown sugar
2 tsp chilli powder

Heat the vinegar and sugar together and bring to the boil to make a thin syrup. Stir in the paste of lime and dates, add the chilli powder and simmer for about 5 minutes. If the chutney is too stiff, you may need to add a little more vinegar. Remove from the heat and, when cool, bottle in sterile jars with non-corrosive lids.

CARROT PICKLE

Gajar Nu Achar

Carrot is a popular vegetable in India, where the most commonly used variety is reddish in colour and quite large. Carrots are employed in a wide range of culinary preparations, from spicy curries to palate-soothing accompaniments such as raitas. Here grated carrot is first sun-dried and then mixed with garlic, ginger and spices and steeped in a malt vinegar. The quantity of vinegar needed will depend on the size of the jars.

1 kg/2 lb peeled carrots

Coarsely grate the carrots and spread them on a flat platter. Cover with muslin or cheesecloth and place in the sun or a warm spot for 3 days, turning over once a day.

3 tsp chilli powder
1 tbsp ground mustard seeds
3 cloves thinly sliced garlic
1 tbsp grated ginger
3 tsp dry-roasted and coarsely ground cumin seeds
1¹/₂ tsp salt

Malt vinegar, sufficient to cover

By the end of the third day, all the moisture should have dried out of the carrot. Place in a bowl and mix in the chilli powder, mustard, garlic, ginger, cumin seeds and salt. Put into jars and pour over sufficient vinegar to cover. Allow to stand for 2 days. You may need to top up the mixture with a little more vinegar if it appears too dry.

PRAWN PICKLE

Colmi Nu Achar

Be warned: this pickle is fiery with chillies and mustard and quite laden with the flavour of garlic – delicious. If you are using pre-cooked prawns, omit the instructions for stir-frying the prawns; simply rinse them and drain well before proceeding with the recipe.

20 dried red chillies
2 cups malt vinegar

Crush the chillies into the vinegar and set aside for a few hours or overnight.

1 kg / 2 lb prawns
2 tsp salt
6 tbsp vegetable oil

Shell and devein the prawns, wash and pat dry. Sprinkle with salt and set aside to drain for 1 hour in a colander.

Heat the oil in a heavy-bottomed pan, drain the prawns and stir-fry until they change colour, taking care to avoid over-cooking. Remove the prawns to a colander to drain and retain the remaining oil.

12 cloves crushed garlic
1 tbsp mustard seeds
1 tbsp cumin seeds
1 tbsp soft brown sugar

Blend the garlic, mustard seeds, cumin seeds and sugar into a paste with the chillies and the vinegar. Re-heat the remaining oil and add the paste. Stir-fry for 2 minutes, add the drained prawns and coat with the masala paste mixture. Remove from the heat and allow to cool. Store in glass jars. Top with oil and stand for 2 days.

DRIED FRUIT PICKLE

Meva Nu Achaar

Traditionally, the sweetening agent used in this recipes would be palm sugar, and I suggest using brown sugar. There are very few hard and fast rules on the making of pickles and chutneys, and almost every family has its own version of a particular preserve, which it claims has been handed down for generations. I have suggested 2 cups of vinegar to cover the fruit, but the quantity needed will vary depending on the size of the bowl.

150 g/5 oz roughly chopped dried figs
150 g/5 oz roughly chopped dried apricots
150 g/5 oz roughly chopped dates
125 g/4 oz roughly chopped sultanas or raisins
2 cups malt vinegar, or enough to cover the fruit

Put the chopped fruits into a glass or ceramic bowl – it is essential that the bowl be non-corrosive. Pour over sufficient vinegar to cover the fruit, cover with cling wrap and allow to steep overnight.

125 g/4 oz soft brown sugar
2 tsp chilli powder
2 tsp salt
2.5 cm/1 inch cinnamon stick
10 cloves
8 bruised cardamom pods
10 peppercorns
1 tsp turmeric powder
4 cm/1¹/₂ inches grated ginger

Drain the vinegar into an enamelled or non-corrosive pan, add the sugar, chilli powder and salt and bring to the boil. Stir in the steeped fruit with any liquid. Add the cinnamon, cloves, cardamom, peppercorns, turmeric and grated ginger. Simmer for 5 minutes and stir to avoid sticking. Discard the cinnamon stick. Remove the cardamom pods and release any seeds remaining in the pods back into the pickle; discard the casings. Remove from the heat and allow to cool before bottling in sterile jars with non-metallic lids.

BOMBAY DUCK CHUTNEY

Boomla Ni Chutney

Bombay Duck is a popular ingredient in chutneys and pickles, but beware – the dried fish gives off a very pungent smell when cooking, and the kitchen window should be kept wide open. Bombay Duck is often sold ready-filleted, and, although I have suggested removing the backbone you may, if you find whole fish, prefer to leave them intact, as the bones are edible.

---

20 dried Bombay Ducks
3 tbsp vegetable oil

Wash the Bombay Ducks, pat them dry and remove their backbones. Heat the oil in a heavy-bottomed frying pan and cook the fish until crisp, taking care that they don't burn. Remove to absorbent paper, leaving the remaining oil in the pan.

---

8 dried red chillies, crushed
2 tsp ground mustard seeds
2 cloves garlic
6 tbsp malt vinegar
Salt to taste

Blend the chillies, ground mustard seeds, garlic, vinegar and salt to a paste in a food-processor. Re-heat the remaining oil, add the paste and stir-fry for 2 minutes. Remove from the source of heat.

Roughly chop the Bombay Ducks and stir into the paste mixture. When cool, blend the Bombay Ducks and masala to a rough paste in a food-processor. Store in glass jars.

INDEX

MOGHUL COOKING

India's Courtly Cuisine

Joyce Westrip

The Moghuls gave India the Taj Mahal and, as this ground-breaking book shows, they also transformed the country's cooking. Duck with cherries, pomegranate soup, apricot-flavoured lamb, aubergines with tamarind: India's Moghul invaders revolutionised the cooking of the subcontinent by bringing from Muslim Persia a refined and sophisticated Middle Eastern cuisine and combining it with Indian spices and ingredients to produce some of the world's boldest food combinations and most exquisite recipes.

Moghul Cooking is the first ever book on the subject and offers the reader a truly mouth-watering selection of dishes. Covering a wide range of recipes from snacks and soups to breads and rice dishes, Joyce Westrip, who was born and brought up in India, also tells the reader how to make sherbets and other drinks and the chutneys and other accompaniments essential for a complete Moghul meal.

Moghul Cooking is not just a book packed with delicious recipes – it is also a fascinating contribution to our understanding of culinary history. The Moghuls are famous for giving India its greatest architectural monuments, for the refinement of their court and its arts: Joyce Westrip establishes that their gifts to Indian cuisine were every bit as important.

'Fascinating ... recipes that are both sumptuous and
easy to follow'
Saveur

paperback

BENGALI COOKING

Seasons and Festivals

Chitrita Banerji

We are only just beginning to appreciate the culinary diversity of the Indian subcontinent's numerous regions. Bengal is home to both Hindus and Muslims and her people farm the fertile Ganges delta for rice and vegetables and fish the region's myriad rivers. As recipes for fish in yoghurt sauce, chicken with poppy seeds, aubergine with tamarind, duck with coconut milk and other delights in *Bengali Cooking* all testify, Bengal has one of Asia's most delicious and distinctive cuisines.

This highly original book takes the reader into kitchens in both Bangladesh and the Indian state of West Bengal by way of the seasons and religious and other festivals that have shaped the region's cooking. Chitrita Banerji offers her readers the wonderful recipes of Bengali home-cooking – dals, fish, vegetables and kedgerees – rather than the standard fare of Indian restaurants. Hers is much more than a cookbook: it is also a vivid and deeply felt introduction to the life, landscape and culture of the Bengali people.

'Delightful ... written with a rare grace and zest'
Matthew Fort, *The Guardian*

'Chitrita Banerji gives her readers a keen appetite for the subtle flavours of India's most interesting region'
Paul Levy

paperback

CASABLANCA CUISINE

French North African Cooking

Aline Benayoun

Casablanca Cuisine recreates the lost world of the *pieds noirs*, French settlers in North Africa, and is a perfect example of food as the meeting point of cultures. Offering such delights as chicken with olives, tuna with red peppers and capers, and date and almond nougat, this is the first ever book on this healthy and sophisticated cuisine.

Borrowing ideas and ingredients from their Arab neighbours, the *pieds noirs* learned to cook meat with fruit and created delicacies such as lamb with pears, chicken with quinces, and meatballs with lemon. Combining European vegetables with a North African spice, they made a beetroot and carrot salad with cumin, while in concocting a mint soup they took the most typical of local herbs and made a refreshing soup of the classic French style.

Like all North African cuisines, *pied noir* cooking places great importance on fresh ingredients, and Aline Benayoun presents a full range of tasty and nutritious vegetable, fish and meat dishes as well as salads and *pied noir* versions of couscous.

'Written from the heart, a delightful book about family cooking with all the tantalising flavours of Morocco. It is also a precious record of the vanished world of the *pied noir* communities of North Africa.'
Claudia Roden

paperback